William
THE BAPTIST

William THE BAPTIST

A Classic Story of a Man's Journey to Understand Baptism

James M. Chaney

Updated by
Ronald Evans

P&R
PUBLISHING
P.O. BOX 817 • PHILLIPSBURG • NEW JERSEY 08865-0817

Library of Congress Cataloging-in-Publication Data

Chaney, James M. (James McDonald), 1831-1909.
  William the Baptist : a classic story of a man's journey to understand baptism / James M. Chaney ; updated by Ronald Evans.
    p. cm.
  Includes bibliographical references and index.
  ISBN 978-1-59638-218-3 (pbk.)
  1. Baptists--Controversial literature. 2. Baptism--Biblical teaching. 3. Baptism--Presbyterian Church. 4. Presbyterian Church--Apologetic works. I. Evans, Ronald, 1947- II. Title.
  BX6334.C5 2011
  234'.161--dc23
                              2011018213

CONTENTS

CONTENTS

FOREWORD

THE LATE DR. ROBERT C. MCQUILKIN, past president
of Columbia Bible College, was asked by an able young Baptist
student, "How do you answer *William the Baptist?*" Dr. McQuilkin
replied, "I don't; I agree with it!" And he continued with the statement that the book should be republished.

I was first introduced to James M. Chaney's *William the Baptist*
over thirty years ago while a student at Westminster Theological
Seminary. It served to validate what I had been taught and had
experienced growing up in a Presbyterian church. So I incorpo-
rated the arguments into my personal theology and practice, put
the book away on my shelf, and went about my Christian life in
an evangelical, nondenominational church.

But it is not easy being a paedobaptist—one who holds to
infant baptism—in an evangelical world that is overwhelmingly
baptistic—holding that only adult believers should be baptized.
(How the majority of evangelicals became baptistic is for another
day.) Recently, the elders of my church wrestled with an issue
related to baptism. It became apparent to me that my fellow elders viewed my baby sprinkling as an uneducated, even unbiblical,
practice. It was not merely that they disagreed with my position,

but that they did not even know there was a biblical justification for infant baptism.

So off to my bookshelf I went to find my copy of *William the Baptist*. My copy was printed in the 1970s by Puritan Reformed Publishers, and was an exact reprint of Dr. McQuilkin's 1877 copy, which had been given to the publisher by James M. Chaney's widow.

Since the literary style and language of 1877 would not communicate well with today's audience, I undertook the discipline of preparing an updated version. In this day of biblical illiteracy, I hope this new edition will reveal to its readers the clear teaching of the Scripture on baptism and its mode and subjects. May it be refreshing and enlightening once again to have *William the Baptist* pose his questions—questions for which there are such satisfying answers.

Ronald B. Evans
Wayne, Pennsylvania
2011

INTRODUCTION

THE BIBLE IS THE BEST WORK on the subject of baptism. In the early part of my ministry, Mr. Staples, a man in my church, introduced me to a Mr. Pruitt, who wished to join the church. I told Mr. Pruitt that the elders were meeting in a few minutes and suggested that he present himself for admission to the church. After a moment's pause, he said, "I have a problem that makes that impossible." Upon inquiry, I found that he believed immersion was the proper mode of baptism. I told him that that was no difficulty; over in Devon there was a Baptist church where he would be welcomed. "But," he said, "I prefer the Presbyterian church for its doctrine."

Mr. Staples proposed to give him some books on the subject of baptism. My reply was, "Mr. Pruitt, let Staples's books alone. If you have set on immersion, my advice to you is to go and unite with the Baptist Church. But if you are not satisfied, take your Bible alone, and examine the subject in light of God's Word, praying for the guidance of the Spirit; after such examination, act according to the conclusion reached."

About four months after this conversation, Mr. Pruitt presented himself to the elders of our church for admission. I asked him whether he was satisfied on the question of baptism. His answer was, "Thoroughly." He proved to be one of the most intelligent Bible Christians I ever knew, and a remarkable witness for the Lord. As I subsequently learned, every influence had been exerted on him to convince him that immersion is baptism.

What people want is a simple exposition of passages in the Bible with which they are familiar. In the following treatise I have confined myself to the Word of God alone, examining the subject by what I conceive to be an exhaustive method, which is:

+ To ascertain the *meaning of the word* used to designate the rite, by examining the context and attending circumstances of each passage.
+ To inquire into the *significance of the rite*, and see what light this throws on the question of mode.
+ To examine the cases of baptism's administration as recorded in the New Testament, in light of *circumstantial evidence*.

I have chosen the conversational method of discussion because it serves better than any other to bring the attention of the reader to the particular point to be impressed on the mind. The only objection to such a method is that it offers the temptation to caricature the views we would assail. I have carefully endeavored to avoid such a weakness.

Much of the heresy prevailing in reference to the rite of baptism is chargeable to the neglect and indifference on the part of those who know and practice baptism the biblical way. It is regrettable that this ordinance is held in such light esteem by some. It is as important as the Lord's Supper. The Lord Jesus instituted both, and each for a specific purpose. If we are unconcerned that men pervert the one, why not the other?

I would not complain of the zeal of any in their opposition to heresies concerning the Lord's Supper. But I would exhort those same contenders to show some measure of zeal against a heresy that would drag the sacred rite of baptism from the place assigned to it by Jesus—as a symbol of the Spirit's work—drag it down to the useless purpose of symbolizing, in a very awkward manner, an event that had *nothing to do* with man's redemption.

If we are in error, let us acknowledge it, and have our practice correspond with the truth. If our practice is in accordance with the command of the Savior, let us not hesitate to affirm that *immersion is not a scriptural mode of baptism.*

Some would object that the view that sprinkling is the only scriptural mode is too extreme, and judge it just as objectionable as the claims of the immersionists that the only scriptural mode is immersion. Moreover, the view of others is that one mode is as good as another, and that it is not a question worthy of discussion. But one must remember what is involved in that position: it implies that the significance of the rite is of no importance. We would not say that of the Lord's Supper. Transubstantiation is not a greater perversion of the Lord's Supper than is the burial theory a perversion of baptism. When immersionists abandon this theory, then they will be in harmony with the simplicity of the gospel.

Rev. James M. Chaney
Lexington, Missouri
1877

1

Domestic Peace

ON A BRIGHT SUMMER EVENING, about the middle of June, as Pastor Cowan was sitting with his wife on their front porch, William Meadows, a promising young lawyer, passed by very leisurely, as if enjoying an evening walk. As the young man reached the gate he seemed, to Pastor Cowan, to indicate a tentative desire to stop—but politely nodding and waving, he passed on. In a few minutes the lawyer returned, and at the gate he repeated these same motions. About fifteen minutes later, Pastor Cowan and his wife saw him again, returning at a more determined and somewhat quicker pace. But his speed slackened as he approached, and after a hasty glance in their direction he turned away toward the opposite side of the street. Then, seeing a friend, William casually crossed the street and began talking with him.

The young man's movements had attracted Pastor Cowan's attention, and he determined to watch and wait. In about ten minutes Mrs. Cowan went inside to see to dinner, and no sooner had she gone than

William hurried across the street to where Pastor Cowan was sitting. The reason for his behavior was soon explained: he wished for Pastor Cowan to attend his marriage, the following week, to Dora Goodling, a young lady who was an active member of Pastor Cowan's church.

Pastor Cowan could not say he was surprised, having already heard speculations about this marriage, and he was neither pleased nor displeased with the announcement. His indifference was not due to anything he knew about his young friend Dora, nor to what he had heard of the young man. William was about twenty-four and from an excellent family. He had obvious intellectual abilities and had graduated with highest honors from one of the best colleges in the country. After that he had attended law school and was now well established in his profession.

But Dora was a Presbyterian, abounding "in every good work" (2 Cor. 9:8), and a most useful member of Pastor Cowan's church. William, by contrast, was a zealous Baptist, though not actually a member of his Baptist church. He was always prepared to argue for the doctrine and its peculiarities, sometimes to a disagreeable extent. Once, at the age of fourteen, he had defended his position in a public discussion on the subject of baptism. Even when others had lost their interest and dropped the discussion, young William's zeal seemed to grow stronger. His passion had given him such a reputation as a defender of Baptist principles that he was commonly known as "William the Baptist." He accepted the nickname as a reward for his youthful fervor. The title stayed with him to such a degree that even in college his professors had also called him "William the Baptist." Even through law school he was known by the nickname.

Regardless, the following week as scheduled, William and Dora were joined as husband and wife, in the sight of God and at the house of a friend. As Pastor Cowan left the wedding, he wondered what sort of life awaited them—she an intelligent, devoted Presbyterian; he, while not yet a member of his church, in principle a zealous Baptist. Pastor Cowan remembered the old question, "Can two walk together except they be agreed?" (Amos 3:3 KJV). There was, humanly speaking, no hope that William would ever join the Presbyterian church, and presumably little chance that Dora would ever consent to become a Baptist.

It seemed that Dora guessed Pastor Cowan's reservations, because two weeks after the wedding she called on him and quickly introduced the subject.

DORA: I'm sure you are curious to know how William and I, with such different beliefs, expect to get along as husband and wife.

PASTOR COWAN: I admit it's been a great concern to me. But it is possible, if you both agree to disagree.

DORA: And that is what we've agreed to do. We discussed it before we got married and agreed not to talk about our differences.

PASTOR COWAN: That should be feasible, as long as both of you can keep to that agreement. But you will find your domestic peace threatened by bitterness and jealousy if you ever decide to pursue your doctrinal differences.

DORA: Don't worry—I've never discussed these issues with anyone, and I have no desire to bring them up with William. I know the arguments this would bring about, and that nothing will change William's beliefs anyway.

Pastor Cowan prayed with Dora before she left, earnestly asking God to bless their marriage and give them a long and happy life together. The couple lived in a house not far from the church, and Pastor and Mrs. Cowan saw Dora almost every day. She continued to attend their church regularly, and William usually accompanied her. Weeks passed, and no couple seemed happier.

2

Agreement to Disagree

The pastor of the Baptist church was an excellent man who was unusually open-minded in his views, reflecting Paul's statement that "Christ did not send me to baptize but to preach the gospel" (1 Cor. 1:17). His church was flourishing, and he was loved and respected by all. He was always ready and willing to join with others in every good work.

Sadly for his congregation, the pastor was so capable that within a year an important church had made an offer to the gifted preacher. Believing that it was God's calling, he left for the larger city and the more extensive sphere of influence. About a year after William and Dora's marriage, a new pastor filled the pulpit of the Baptist church: Pastor Roberts, a learned man who was strong in his views. He was skilled and capable behind the pulpit and was always seeking to bring new members into the church. He visited William and Dora's home frequently, and it was not long before Dora started attending events at the Baptist church.

The new pastor was exerting a definite influence on William, and although Dora still attended the Presbyterian church, she thought that attending the Baptist church with her husband might prompt him to make a *public* confession of his faith in Christ. She had no hope of his becoming a Presbyterian, but her first desire was that he would become a professing Christian. She greatly preferred that he become a member of the Baptist church rather than continue to have no connection to any church.

One evening the new pastor made a short visit to their home, but William was not there and he did not stay long. As Pastor Roberts was about to leave, he made a remark about religious differences between husbands and wives. Jokingly, he asked Dora if she could make a good Presbyterian out of William. Her reply was, "What! William the Baptist? I should think not—I'd be better off trying to make a Presbyterian out of you." This seemed to please Pastor Roberts. So after mentioning how intelligent William was and the importance of his making a public confession of faith (since he showed evidence of being converted), the pastor departed.

The next Sunday night, William asked his wife if she would like to go with him to the Baptist church. She readily agreed. The sermon was on the text, "My servant Caleb . . . has a different spirit and has followed me fully" (Num. 14:24), and was quite good. The preacher showed what it meant to follow the Lord fully and beautifully described the life of one who is devoted, body and soul, to the Lord's service.

At the close, Pastor Roberts very skillfully wove a picture of Christ descending into the Jordan, where he was, by John—as he said, "to fulfill all righteousness" (Matt. 3:15)—to be "buried beneath the wave." The preacher said there were many who desired to follow Christ, and who did follow him in what they thought was the spirit of his commandments, but who did not think it necessary to follow him beneath the wave. They followed him, but unlike Caleb, they did not follow him *fully*. Such persons, the pastor said, should remember the words of the Savior as he was about to enter the watery grave: "For thus it is fitting for us to fulfill all righteousness."

Assuming everybody's agreement that Jesus had entered the watery grave, Pastor Roberts noted that some had persuaded themselves that it was not essential to do the same—that some other mode of baptism would fill the requirement. Again, he reminded his parishioners that Caleb was commended because he followed the Lord fully, and that Jesus himself was immersed in the Jordan "to fulfill all righteousness."

After the benediction, a throng of women came to welcome and trade kind words with William and his wife, making Dora's little arms ache from the many handshakes. The pastor, with a pleasant smile, greeted her and joked, "Remember what I said about your husband. Don't despair; keep trying, and you may succeed." But Dora gave no response. The very thought of opening a discussion with William about their differences filled her with horror. She had no desire to attempt to "make a Presbyterian" out of him, and even less to change her own views.

Early in the fall there was a festival to raise funds to renovate the Baptist church. William suggested to Dora that he would be grateful for her help, and she cheerfully consented. As she did with any good work, she threw herself into it with such gusto that one would have thought she was serving her own church—making some of their Baptist friends misinterpret her enthusiasm. Her efforts at the festival and her frequent attendance at the Baptist church led to the rumor that she and her husband would soon be joining them. Pastor Cowan heard the rumor but believed it to be baseless.

One thing did suggest that Dora might be moving toward the Baptist position: the issue of the baptism of the couple's first child, now about six months old. Pastor Cowan assumed that William had opposed presenting their child for infant baptism, but he expected Dora to at least speak to him and describe why it was impossible for her to fulfill such a pleasing duty of a Presbyterian parent.

Not long after Pastor Cowan came to this conclusion, Dora did visit him. She explained that she had spoken to her husband about the baptism, and the mere suggestion had greatly annoyed him. William expressed his contempt for that "archaic superstition, baby sprinkling!"—hurting Dora's feelings as never before.

At first Dora kept silent and was sorry she had mentioned the child's baptism at all. William soon realized that his words had deeply wounded his wife. After a period of mutual silence he withdrew his objection, since he knew that performing the rite would satisfy Dora and believed it could do the child no harm.

And now Dora had come to seek the advice of her minister, Pastor Cowan. Should she proceed, she wondered, with only grudging permission from her husband? Pastor Cowan told her that if she thought her husband was sincere in encouraging her to baptize their child—even if his motive was only to gratify her—he thought she should do so. As a result, Dora presented her child the next Sunday, and in the ordinance of baptism she dedicated her son to God, taking the vow to bring him up for Jesus. As she wept, many others who knew her circumstances wept with her. From many hearts a silent "Amen" went out as the pastor prayed for the covenant-keeping God to bless the mother and child.

Not long after this, on one of his visits, the Baptist minister asked Dora about her success with "making a good Presbyterian" out of her husband. She told Pastor Roberts that the subject had never been mentioned by either of them, and that doing so would violate the solemn pledge they had made before they were married. While he sympathized with her and agreed that it was a delicate subject, the pastor expressed his fear that these differences were keeping her husband from joining a church. This struck a tender chord in Dora. She believed her husband was a true Christian and had long wished that he would become a member in the congregation of his choice, which she knew to be the Baptist church.

Pastor Roberts voiced the opinion that it was a very unpleasant situation for a husband and wife to be separate, and that he would rather see them together in her church than to see William in no church at all. Dora was pleased with his selfless interest in her husband's spiritual welfare. She thanked him, but pointed out that there was no chance of this happening and that she hoped William would make a public profession of his faith in Christ and join the Baptist church.

Pastor Roberts then suggested that there could be no harm in talking the matter over with William and said he would like to explore whether a compromise could be made. With her consent, he offered to speak to William and urge him to have such a discussion with her. She thanked the pastor and they agreed that he would speak to William and arrange for them to meet.

A few days later, Dora was surprised to hear William bring up the subject as they were sitting together after dinner. He told her that it had been his desire to become a member of a church, but that he had been greatly troubled by the doctrinal differences between them, and had not mentioned it because of their pledge. He was willing to do whatever it took to resolve their differences, but he thought it would require less sacrifice for her to go with him to the Baptist church than for him to go with her to the Presbyterian.

Dora saw fresh troubles in this suggestion. She could not be received into the Baptist church without repudiating her baptism—something she could not and would not do. But she did not want to argue the matter. She wished she had not given her permission for the issue to be discussed, but what could she do? She had to give an answer. After a moment's pause Dora told William that she thought they had better not discuss the subject, but should continue as they had promised before marriage: to agree to disagree. And she urged him to apply at once for admission into the Baptist church.

William was not prepared for such a response. He wanted to discuss the matter; he felt sure he could convince Dora that he was right and that she should go with him to the Baptist church. Since she was so opposed to talking it over he thought he had better drop the subject, but he could not dismiss it from his mind. He was sure he could bring her to acknowledge her error if he could go over the whole subject of baptism.

William's difficulties had seemed to increase, and though he had approached the subject with hope, he now despaired. After failing to put the issue out of his mind, he left for a walk. Before he knew it he was at the home of Pastor Roberts, where he told the Baptist minister his troubles. William compared his situation to that of the Israelites: they had explained their difficulties in the hope of getting relief, but afterward their condition was worse than before. He described his recent conversation with his wife and the result of that conversation. "Now what should I do?" he queried.

PASTOR ROBERTS: Don't despair; "let patience have her perfect work" (James 1:4 KJV). Did you tell Dora that you would join her church?

WILLIAM: No, I didn't. I would join the Presbyterians *only* if they would immerse me. But I know they won't.

PASTOR ROBERTS: I've known Presbyterian ministers, though, who would immerse a desirable member rather than turn him away.

WILLIAM: Not Pastor Cowan!

PASTOR ROBERTS: Perhaps his refusal will have the right effect on your wife. It will help her to see how unreasonable and uncompromising their position is, and might convince her to come with you to the Baptist congregation.

William was encouraged. He felt sure that he would be safe in offering to join Dora's church on the condition that he be immersed. If Pastor Cowan refused, then it would be a powerful argument for her to come with him. He quickly walked home. Sitting down beside Dora, he found himself hoping more resolutely than ever that his troubles would soon be over, and that his wife would be with him in the church of his choice.

After some pleasant conversation, William announced, "Dora, I have some good news for you. Since it's impossible for you to become a Baptist, I have decided to apply for membership in your church."

Dora was startled. She was not prepared for such an announcement and did not know what to think or say. At last she murmured, "I think you may have reached this decision too hastily." Now it was William's turn to be surprised. He had expected her response to be one of joy. After a little pause to recover from his astonishment, William said gently, "Dearest, I don't understand you; please explain what you mean."

"I mean," Dora began, "that doctrine should be based only on our beliefs, not on a desire to please someone else—even if it's

23

your mother, father, husband, or wife. Do you remember what Paul says in Galatians 1:10? 'Am I now seeking the approval of man, or of God? Or am I trying to please man? If I were still trying to please man, I would not be a servant of Christ.' In matters of biblical teaching, we sometimes have to disagree with our fathers, mothers, husbands, and wives."

Every word Dora spoke served to increase William's astonishment. All of a sudden, his hope was not as bright as it had been just a short time before. *But*, he thought, *she must hear my proposal.*

WILLIAM: Dora, I have thought carefully about this. As I said, I'm ready to make almost any sacrifice in order to be with you at church. As you know, I prefer the Baptist church, but I can live in the Presbyterian church in good conscience, too. They don't require their members to subscribe to all their doctrines—I heard your pastor say so from his pulpit not long ago.

DORA: But William, what about your baptism?

WILLIAM: That's the only problem, and it's a very small one. Since I am willing to meet more than halfway in this compromise, your pastor shouldn't be unreasonable enough to refuse me one small favor. I know some Presbyterian ministers who would agree to immerse.

For her part, however, Dora saw no solution to their troubles. She did not believe that Pastor Cowan would grant William's request. In fact, from her own brief examination of the subject, she strongly questioned whether a Presbyterian minister could, with consistency of conscience, perform baptism by immersion at all.

Dora kept these views to herself to avoid a discussion, but she did tell her husband that, in all probability, he would be disappointed if he were counting on Pastor Cowan to immerse him. But

William insisted that they meet with him so they could explain their differences and so that he could apply for membership. Dora reluctantly agreed but felt that the discussion would not have a good outcome. In fact, she greatly feared that it would make matters worse. She was certain that Pastor Cowan would refuse to immerse William, and that this would only make her husband more determined in his opposition to her church.

3

WHICH CHURCH AND HOW?

THE FOLLOWING MONDAY EVENING the visit took place. William and Dora found Pastor Cowan in a good mood from having just spent time with his children, though the little ones looked disappointed that the couple's arrival had put an end to their playtime with their father. Pastor Cowan explained that Monday was his rest day, on which he usually took the opportunity to be with his children. William and Dora began to wonder if they were intruding. But soon Mrs. Cowan came and took the children to another part of the house, and they felt perfectly at ease once it became apparent that the children had forgotten the intrusion.

William's mind was so full of thoughts about the visit that he did not want to delay introducing his subject. But he was at a loss as to how to begin. On the previous day six new members had been added to the Presbyterian church, so William started by commenting on the spiritual interest evident in Pastor Cowan's congregation. In reply the minister related some of the new members' conversion experiences and expressed the hope that there would be a spiritual awakening in the community. Then, greatly to William's relief, the minister addressed him personally.

PASTOR COWAN: William, I've been wondering for some time why you haven't addressed your own spiritual condition.

WILLIAM: I have been giving it a lot of thought for quite a while. The last several months, it's been bothering me a great deal.

PASTOR COWAN: The matter is very simple. Your condition as a sinner is evident, and your only hope is to accept the Lord Jesus as your Savior.

WILLIAM: I believe I already have. I know my only hope is his righteousness.

PASTOR COWAN: Then you are a Christian. We are all the children of God by faith in Christ Jesus, and it is pleading the righteousness of Jesus that secures our acceptance.

WILLIAM: My problem is that I haven't made a public profession of my faith in Jesus.

PASTOR COWAN: Your sense of duty is appropriate; this should be done as soon as possible.

WILLIAM: You're right—I have put it off far too long. But now I don't know what to do.

PASTOR COWAN: Well, why the delay?

WILLIAM: I have a problem on the subject of baptism. My take on the issue is that I should follow the Savior fully and be immersed.

PASTOR COWAN: And what is stopping you? I don't see how this is a problem. I have often thought what a blessing it is that there are different churches to accommodate people with different views. You will find the Baptist church perfectly suited to your views. And if you'll take my advice, I suggest you apply for membership as soon as you can.

WILLIAM: But my wife is a member of your church, and I can't bear the thought of being separated from her. I have come to believe in the importance of a family worshiping together—don't you think we should be with each other?

PASTOR COWAN: Of course I do, but under the current circumstances I don't see how this is possible. For your wife to be immersed against her convictions, or for you to have water poured out on you while you believe immersion is the only true baptism—either situation would be even worse.

Just then the pastor's wife returned and suggested that William read a small pamphlet on the subject of baptism. But Pastor Cowan said, "No, I would advise against that. If you are already as set in your views as you seem to be, I think the best thing would be to go to the Baptist church and apply for admission. If, however, your views on baptism are not settled, then turn to the Bible and examine the subject in light of God's Word alone, asking for the guidance of the Holy Spirit." William listened attentively, pausing only briefly.

WILLIAM: I don't need to examine the subject; my views are fixed. I got them from the Word of God, and there's no argument anyone can use to change my mind. I can think of only one solution.

PASTOR COWAN: What's that?

WILLIAM: For you to immerse me.

PASTOR COWAN: That's something I cannot do, without doing as much damage to my conscience as you would to yours if you were baptized our way.

WILLIAM: Then there's nothing we can do?

PASTOR COWAN: Well, there is one way it can still work.

WILLIAM: And what is that?

PASTOR COWAN: Join the Baptist church, then get a certificate of membership and apply for admission into our church.

William was thoroughly pleased at this idea of Pastor Cowan's and wondered why he had not thought of it. He was determined to unite at once with the Baptist church, gain a certificate of membership, and then apply for membership in the Presbyterian Church. The question that had troubled him for so long seemed at last to be solved, and he was very glad that he had met with Pastor Cowan.

The next evening William met with Pastor Roberts. His cheerful countenance attested that he had been released from his burden. His pastor interpreted this as a favorable sign and greeted him with similar cheerfulness.

WILLIAM: I think the question that has been bothering me for so long has finally been solved.

PASTOR ROBERTS: Did Pastor Cowan agree to immerse you?

WILLIAM: Oh, no—in fact, he very clearly refused, and advised me, since my views are fixed, to join the Baptist church.

PASTOR ROBERTS: This is better advice than I expected him to give. I'm surprised he didn't give you a dozen books to read, to try to convince you that sprinkling is true baptism.

WILLIAM: No—Mrs. Cowan suggested that, but he opposed the idea and said I should go to the Bible alone.

PASTOR ROBERTS: Really? That surprises me as much as his suggestion that you join our church. He knows perfectly well that there is no evidence for baptism in the Bible apart from immersion. Very strange advice. Dora saw how unreasonable it was that he refused to immerse you, didn't she?

WILLIAM: No, we didn't say anything about that. Pastor Cowan gave a very good reason for refusing.

PASTOR ROBERTS: Well, has Dora agreed to join with you?

WILLIAM: No, she hasn't—I haven't even asked her about it.

PASTOR ROBERTS: Then I don't see how your problem has been solved.

WILLIAM: Here's how: I have decided to be immersed and to join your church, and you can give me a certificate of membership. That way I can take it to the Presbyterian church and be admitted there.

PASTOR ROBERTS: Well, that's certainly *one* solution. . . . How did you get this idea?

WILLIAM: Pastor Cowan suggested it.

PASTOR ROBERTS: Ah, I should have suspected as much—but I'm surprised that a man of your intelligence didn't see the glaring inconsistency in what he said. One minute he decisively refuses to immerse you, and the next he agrees to accept your immersion, as long as *I* administer it, as a valid baptism. Do you see how grossly inconsistent that is?

WILLIAM: I admit I didn't before; but now that you mention it, it does seem odd. I'm sorry I didn't ask him to explain it more clearly. But I'm still willing to proceed on those terms if he is.

PASTOR ROBERTS: Well, I, for one, am not willing to take part in anything so underhanded!

WILLIAM: You won't immerse me?

PASTOR ROBERTS: In a word, no! But if you want my advice, meet with him and listen to his views on baptism, and point out to him the inconsistency of his position. Take Dora with you so that she can see firsthand how contradictory his opinions are. Mark my words, everything will work out.

William left, returning home as depressed as he had previously been elated. Dora noticed his gloomy appearance. She wondered what was the matter but was too afraid to ask. He sat quietly for some time, lost in thought. At last he broke the silence.

WILLIAM: Well, my dear, the problem I thought we had solved is no closer to a solution after all.

DORA: What happened? Did Pastor Roberts convince you not to join my church?

WILLIAM: No, nothing like that.

DORA: Did he tell you to convince me to join his?

WILLIAM: No, he didn't say that either.

DORA: Then what's the trouble? What did he say?

WILLIAM: He positively refuses to immerse me so that I can join the Presbyterian church, and I'm beginning to think that he's right. Don't you see how inconsistent it is for Pastor Cowan to refuse to immerse me but to still accept the letter of transfer from the Baptist church? I'm astonished that I didn't think of it myself.

DORA: But it's customary for Presbyterians to receive anyone from a Baptist church who applies for membership without re-baptizing them.

WILLIAM: But think of how inconsistent it is. I ought to talk with Pastor Cowan and explain it to him. He should never give advice like that again, for his own sake.

DORA: Please, William, let's drop the subject and say nothing. This has given us nothing but trouble from the start. I was afraid of this from the beginning, and I'm sorry now that I gave Pastor

Roberts my approval to talk to you. Please—I wish you would put this out of your mind. Say no more to Pastor Cowan; just go and join the Baptist church, and pray that God will bless us both.

WILLIAM: I think you're right. I see now there is no possible way we can be together in the same church. I will follow your advice, but I must show Pastor Cowan the inconsistency of his position first. Churches should be free from any sign of deceit; he needs to understand and acknowledge this. I will try to get him to explain his position on baptism—especially the way he proposed it—but *from the Bible alone*. He doesn't seem to have given it much thought. And I think it would be good if I convinced him of the reasons to be immersed.

A few days later, William saw Pastor Cowan in town. He told him that he had changed his mind on the idea of joining the Baptist church in order to get a certificate for the Presbyterian church. "With your permission," he continued, "I would like to have a conversation with you on the whole subject of baptism. I could come to your office any evening that's convenient and go over the subject with you."

Pastor Cowan did not act surprised at this change, nor did he ask what had caused it. He suggested that William come to his home instead of his office, and also indicated that one evening would probably not be enough. They agreed that William would come to his house on the following Monday evening.

4

First Evening: Valid, But Not Scriptural

On Monday evening, after an early supper, William and Dora hurried to Pastor Cowan's house. Dora wanted to stay home, but William had insisted that she accompany him. They found the minister ready to receive them. After mutual greetings, William, impatient to begin, opened the discussion as Dora listened quietly.

William: I am here to discuss baptism. I should tell you up front: I am thoroughly convinced that the only true mode of baptism is immersion. I don't think it is possible to convince me that anything else meets the requirements of Christ's command. But since I am anxious to join your church so I can be with my wife, and since you refuse to immerse me, I thought I would at least talk with you to see what other possible solutions there are. First, let me ask you why you refuse to immerse me.

PASTOR COWAN: I'm glad you have come, first of all. I appreciate the opportunity to answer your question, especially since some people are under the impression that Presbyterians are not as consistent as we should be with regard to baptism. A thorough conversation on the subject can do no harm. The answer to your question of why I refuse to immerse you is very simple. It's because I do not believe immersion is the scriptural mode of baptism.

WILLIAM: I'm confused; I thought you believed that immersion is scriptural but is not essential.

PASTOR COWAN: No—if that were my view, I would happily agree to your request. I refused because I do not believe that immersion is a scriptural mode of administering baptism. It fails, in essential ways, to meet the requirements of baptism as instituted and appointed by Christ.

WILLIAM: Well, this is certainly new to me! In fact, last Sunday I heard Pastor Roberts preach a sermon strongly supporting immersion as the method recognized by every denomination. But how do you reconcile this theory with your practice? You offered to receive me once I was immersed—suggested that I have Pastor Roberts immerse me and then come to you with a certificate of membership, which you would accept.

PASTOR COWAN: Yes, it is customary for us to receive anyone from an evangelical church who applies for membership and to accept his immersion—that is, if the person is entirely satisfied that it is a valid baptism.

WILLIAM: Well, this seems irreconcilable to me. It can be valid but not scriptural? Not scriptural but valid? If you can sort out this contradiction, I think it will help me clarify my views about the mode of baptism.

PASTOR COWAN: Well, if those conclusions contradict each other, then they are definitely irreconcilable, and that would mean that our theory and practice are inconsistent. But let me ask you: what do you mean by "valid"?

WILLIAM: Something is valid if it meets the requirements of the gospel and the commands of Christ.

PASTOR COWAN: Very good. But maybe we'll understand each other better if we consider "validity" as it applies to some other situations. What would you say is the scriptural way to administer and celebrate the Lord's Supper?

WILLIAM: I believe the method you practice in your church agrees with what Christ instituted.

PASTOR COWAN: Then it is scriptural?

WILLIAM: Yes, I believe it is.

PASTOR COWAN: And as instituted by Christ and celebrated by the apostles, do you think the Lord's Supper involved kneeling while they were partaking of the elements?

WILLIAM: No, sir—in fact, I am fairly certain that they didn't kneel. And I admit, I've wondered about the appropriateness of celebrating Communion that way, since it seems to have no basis in the Word of God.

PASTOR COWAN: You believe it is unscriptural?

WILLIAM: Yes.

PASTOR COWAN: Do you think it destroys the character of the celebration as the Lord's Supper altogether? Can the opponents of this mode claim that it is disqualified from being the Lord's Supper at all?

WILLIAM: Well, I wouldn't go that far. It's just that it takes away from the simplicity of the Lord's Supper that Christ instituted and has no basis in Scripture.

PASTOR COWAN: I see—so it is unscriptural, but it may be valid.

WILLIAM: I think that "valid" fits in this case. Since the bread and wine are still given and received, the essentials of the Supper are still there.

PASTOR COWAN: Very true—and it's the same way with immersionists. By using water in baptism, they keep the essential element, but they have no scriptural basis for their *mode* of using it. Now, this doesn't necessarily make their baptism invalid. But even though I consider baptisms by immersion to be valid, it would be wrong for me to deliberately administer a mode that I believe to be unscriptural.

WILLIAM: Your argument sounds convincing, but can you give me another illustration of your point?

PASTOR COWAN: As many as you wish—in fact, as many as the number of external elements in a worship service. In all of these externals, God looks at the heart and considers the spirit in which the service is offered. Let me ask you what you regard as the scriptural Sabbath day.

WILLIAM: Sunday, by universal agreement.

PASTOR COWAN: Would it be proper or scriptural for you or your church to change it to another day without scriptural authority?

WILLIAM: No, I don't think that would be allowed.

PASTOR COWAN: The situation is a very realistic one. Let's suppose that some Christian missionaries are deep in the jungle for many months and lose track of the days of the week. Sunday comes, and they all carry out their usual work. Now, by their count, Monday becomes the Lord's Day, and they observe it as such for many weeks. Unintentionally they have changed the Lord's Day (the first day of the week) to Monday. It's unscriptural to substitute Monday for the day that Christ appointed, but we would all agree that under the circumstances, their celebration on Monday meets all the requirements of the gospel.

WILLIAM: That makes sense. And it reconciles what I thought was irreconcilable. It certainly agrees with what Christ said in John 4:24: "God is spirit, and those who worship him must worship in spirit and truth." In external things, God considers the intention and the spirit of the people who perform them.

PASTOR COWAN: Another example is the installation of elders, which has a lot in common with the issue of receiving people from evangelical churches who have already been immersed. We believe that elders should be installed by the laying on of hands, according to 1 Timothy 4:14. To set men apart for their work without this ceremony would be unscriptural. But suppose, through some accident (which might happen in a busy church), the laying on of hands in one case was overlooked, and an elder began his duties without it. If, after some time had gone by, the mistake was realized, would that mean that all his official acts were null and void?

WILLIAM: No, of course not. The elder's installation may have been improper, but it was not invalid. I see now—this scenario is the same as the previous one. Now I understand how you can accept immersion but refuse to administer it yourself. It's the same as accepting the incomplete installation of an elder as valid without deliberately taking part in it.

PASTOR COWAN: So you see how I can receive someone who has been immersed even though it would be wrong for me to immerse someone?

WILLIAM: I can see that now. But I'm still amazed that you consider immersion to be an unscriptural mode of baptism. You won't find many people who agree with your extreme position.

PASTOR COWAN: Immersionists are zealous in their efforts to give that impression, but I'm afraid they are zealously wrong. Most of the ministers in our denomination agree with me. Admittedly, a few of them see the mode as merely external and are indifferent about it, and in their lack of conviction they sometimes make concessions that immersionists notice and use to their advantage. I've known some Presbyterians who would administer the sacrament that way if they were asked to, even though they believed immersion to be an unscriptural mode of baptism.

William: This is new to me. Aren't you underestimating the number of them who make concessions? I've heard many sermons by immersionists that give the impression that all paedobaptists make these kinds of concessions.

Pastor Cowan: Most immersionists make those concessions their main point when they argue their position against Presbyterians. Several years ago I heard a Baptist minister offer to discuss the subject from a purely biblical viewpoint. Unfortunately, all he had managed to do after five hours was explain the meaning of *báptizō*, using Greek lexicons and the commentary of some misguided paedobaptists. The Bible itself never came up!

William: Are you saying that a paedobaptist can make a case for infant baptism using the Bible alone?

Pastor Cowan: Do you think any other method would be legitimate or satisfactory?

William: No, I think that would be the best way to accomplish it.

Pastor Cowan: Then my answer is a definite "Yes!" The Bible affirms this method in Isaiah 8:20: "To the teaching and to the testimony! If they will not speak according to this word, it is because they have no dawn [light]."

William: I would be delighted to hear someone try to oppose the arguments for immersion, and to show me a command that "the Lord God said" (Gen. 2:18) in favor of sprinkling!

PASTOR COWAN: Believe me, it would be my pleasure to satisfy you. But I think we should postpone our discussion and start again on another evening, since it's getting late now.

WILLIAM: I hope I can come back soon; you have piqued my curiosity by what you're proposing to do. This all seems too incredible—attempting to overturn the whole position of immersion, and establishing sprinkling *by the Bible alone* as the scriptural mode!

PASTOR COWAN: If you are available, I'll look forward to your visit on Thursday night.

5

Second Evening: From Quantity to Action

When Thursday evening came, William did not insist that Dora come with him, but went to Pastor Cowan's house by himself. This seemed best, especially in light of a conversation he had had with Pastor Roberts the day before.

WILLIAM: Excuse me, sir, for being so early, but my curiosity got the best of me. I saw Pastor Roberts and told him about our meeting, and he made a suggestion, which I mentioned to Dora, that she apply for membership in the Baptist church and be immersed. But before we talk about that, I want to ask you a question. I hope you will answer without letting your denomination speak for you, and will remember that Dora's and my spiritual lives are at stake. I won't mention the question to Dora unless you agree that it's okay to do so. The question is, wouldn't it be easier for Dora to go with me to the Baptist church than for me to become a Presbyterian, especially since you refuse to immerse me?

PASTOR COWAN: I am glad you came early, and just as glad to see that your interest has not slackened. Thank you for your confidence in me to give an opinion that rises above my denominational preferences. I will try to answer you as our Lord would want me to answer. This suggestion Pastor Roberts gave you makes me question his understanding of the consequences if Dora took such an action. Do you believe that Dora is an honest, intelligent Christian woman?

WILLIAM: Without a doubt, in all respects.

PASTOR COWAN: Well then, as a member of the Presbyterian church, she believes she has already been baptized according to the command of Christ. Let me give you an illustration. Twelve years ago a nominal Catholic named Alan Low married a member of the Presbyterian church named Sandy Dean. The ceremony was performed by a Presbyterian minister. Things went smoothly for three or four years, until Alan's priest convinced him to become much more zealous in his beliefs. The priest told him that he was not lawfully married, and that he was committing a great sin to continue in that state. He insisted that Alan be remarried according to the laws of the Catholic church.

Sandy was informed of this and was asked to agree to the marriage. Her answer was quick and decisive: "No! Never!" She saw the suggestion as casting contempt on her own church. It would mean admitting that her church was apostate and that its ministers were impostors with no authority to validate a marriage. It would be confessing that she had been living in adultery all those years. What do you think of her conclusions and her answer?

WILLIAM: I believe she was right and an honest Christian.

PASTOR COWAN: And what would Dora be saying if she agreed to Pastor Roberts's suggestion? What if she applied to join the Baptist church and was immersed? Wouldn't she be confessing that her church is really not a church, and that its ministers have no authority to administer the sacraments? Even if she didn't hold these views, wouldn't her actions pour contempt on the sacrament of baptism—treating it as so common and of such little worth that she could freely prostitute it just to gain the approval of the man she loves?

WILLIAM: I see now that I wasn't thinking clearly—I can understand what a mistake it would be for her to take this step. I won't agree to put her through this, then, unless there is a radical transformation in her views on baptism.

PASTOR COWAN: I'm glad to hear you say that, William. Now, before we proceed, we should have a clear understanding of what we will be studying. What do you understand baptism, or "immersion," to mean?

WILLIAM: Well, it's very simple. It means putting the person *down into* the water, and taking him *up out of* the water, in the name of the Father, the Son, and the Holy Spirit.

PASTOR COWAN: Very good. Here's another question: would the requirement be met if enough water to cover the person were *poured* on him instead?

WILLIAM: Definitely not; that would be inadequate and unacceptable. There would be no immersion that way—no *putting down into* or *taking up out of*.

PASTOR COWAN: Of course your answer is correct. The whole difference between the Presbyterians and the immersionists is not in the *element* that is used, nor in *how much* of it is used; we agree on those points. Where we disagree is in the action of *how* the water is applied. With the immersionists, the individual must be *put into* the water; with us, the water must be *applied to* the individual. That difference is radical. And now we can start considering the question.

WILLIAM: Yes, sir. And let's start with the understanding that only the Bible is to be brought forward as evidence. No Greek, no commentaries, no creeds or catechisms. I'm assuming that is your intention—I see you have only your Bible with you.

PASTOR COWAN: Correct—with only one stipulation. I wouldn't say we should ignore the Greek altogether. I do propose that we confine ourselves exclusively to the Bible; however, a portion of the Bible was written in the Greek language. So, even though the meaning of the Greek word that gives us our word *baptism* must be determined by its use in the Bible, this can't be done without referencing the original language.

WILLIAM: That makes sense—what I meant was that you would not use quotations from classical Greek authors.

PASTOR COWAN: I agree. The best way to understand the meaning of a specific word that appears frequently in any book is to look carefully at how it is used in the instances throughout that book.

WILLIAM: I don't understand—I thought the best way would be to consult the dictionaries of that language. Or, if there is a root for the word you are studying, to consider that when analyzing the word's meaning.

PASTOR COWAN: Well, putting too much emphasis on how the word is derived might lead to error. For example, our word *prevent* is derived from the Latin preposition *prae*, meaning "before," and *venire*, meaning "to come." Therefore, the word *prevent* should mean "to come before." But this meaning has long been obsolete. Words undergo changes in meaning over time.

As for dictionaries, how do you suppose the compilers get their information? The lexicographer assigns a meaning to a word. Then, to back up that meaning, he quotes passages from standard authors in which the word occurs. He determines the meaning from context and circumstantial evidence—in other words, from the word's usage.

WILLIAM: That's a legitimate conclusion. But how does establishing a word's meaning that way prove that *baptism* doesn't mean "immersion"?

PASTOR COWAN: As we examine the Bible, we need only look at those passages where the context or surrounding circumstances throw some light on the meaning of the word as used by the writer. For instance, consider the Great Commission: "Go therefore and make disciples of all nations, baptizing them in the name of the Father and of the Son and of the Holy Spirit" (Matt. 28:19). Though the word *báptizō* occurs, the context doesn't give any clues to its meaning.

Also, there are many passages where our word occurs, from which no conclusions can be drawn without long, tedious discussions about the significance of the prepositions. For example, John said, "I baptize with water" (John 1:26). The meaning of *baptize* here depends on the meaning of the preposition *with*; on its own, the English would imply that the water was *applied* to the people.

Or consider "Jesus . . . was baptized by John in the Jordan" (Mark 1:9). Here the simple facts determine nothing about the meaning of *baptize*: once John and Jesus went into the water, John may have performed the rite by either dipping or sprinkling. Passages like these must be examined in conjunction with other evidence.

WILLIAM: Don't the circumstances surrounding the baptism of Jesus, which you just mentioned, along with the baptism of the Ethiopian eunuch, both point to immersion?

PASTOR COWAN: After we consider the meaning of the word, then we will examine the most important passages dealing with how baptism was performed. Right now, let's look at the passages where the use of the word clearly indicates its meaning. Please turn to Mark 7:4: "When they come from the marketplace, they [the Jews] do not eat unless they wash. And there are many other traditions that they observe, such as the washing of cups and pots and copper vessels and dining couches."

Here in the Greek the same word used to indicate baptism, *báptizō*, is used and translated as "wash." The passage says that the Jews washed themselves *and* their household items, including couches (in the earliest manuscripts). Every time they came from the marketplace they "baptized." It's possible that they might have immersed themselves to do this, but it takes imagination to see it as probable. Even so, their purpose was to *purify* or *cleanse* themselves. We know they were in the habit of doing this.

WILLIAM: You admit that they could have immersed themselves, so I don't see how the word as it's used here serves your purpose.

PASTOR COWAN: If you turn to John 2:6, you'll find an account of how exactly they washed themselves and their household furniture. Here we have a detailed description of Christ's first miracle, turning the water into wine at the marriage in Cana. In verse 6 we read, "Now there were six stone water jars there for the Jewish rites of purification, each holding twenty or thirty gallons." Even if we consider the jar with the largest amount, thirty gallons, the Jews could not possibly have immersed themselves, much less their couches.

WILLIAM: I see. And I admit that comparing these passages raises a point that I hadn't considered before you called it to my attention.

PASTOR COWAN: The dining couches, in particular, are very telling. It would take a powerful imagination to picture how they might have been immersed! This is for two reasons. First, their size: they would be far too cumbersome for any ordinary housewife to consider immersing them. Second, there is no sensible reason why any housewife would want to immerse them. Immersion is not a requirement for cleaning anything. Sure, cups and pots are sometimes immersed in the process of cleaning, but this is an unintended consequence. The usual method is to run water over them while rubbing or partially dipping them. But whoever heard of immersing chairs and tables in order to clean them?

WILLIAM: I freely admit that immersion is not actually taking place here. But this means nothing to my argument—because, by being washed all over, weren't the couches still technically enveloped with water? Couldn't the washing figuratively be considered baptism or immersion? The end result, either way, is that they were enveloped.

PASTOR COWAN: I will make this concession on one condition—that we regard it from this point on as a fixed position that we both agree on and can refer to as such later.

WILLIAM: That condition sounds fair—I accept it.

PASTOR COWAN: Then let me call your attention to a definition you gave. I asked you to define *immersion*, because without a definition, any discussion would be useless.

WILLIAM: And I gave a definition that applied to carrying out the rite itself—to real immersion.

PASTOR COWAN: But now we have to find the meaning of the word used to designate the rite. So far it seems that the word used in the Bible denotes a different action from *putting down into* and *taking up out of*.

WILLIAM: I'll have to think about this—at this point I'm not ready to give an opinion on it.

Pastor Cowan: Go ahead and think about it, and let me ask you another question. If pouring water over a table could figuratively, as you say, "baptize" it, then would you agree that if I used a hyssop branch or my hand to sprinkle enough water over an individual so that he would be enveloped in it, this would also be a figurative immersion or baptism?

William: This sounds like the point I have already agreed to, but maybe I was rash to agree in the first place.

Pastor Cowan: Why are you changing your mind?

William: Because otherwise I would have to acknowledge that real baptism, according to the Bible's use of the word, could be performed without immersion at all, by simply applying water to the person or thing being baptized.

Pastor Cowan: I'm glad you understand the point so clearly.

William: I admit, I'm very perplexed. Since I was a boy I've been very interested in the subject, and everything I've read has convinced me that nothing could change my mind on it. When I set up this appointment, I secretly hoped to convince *you* of *your* error. Now it's giving me pause, because I haven't heard the arguments you're presenting before.

Pastor Cowan: Maybe it's because your reading has always been on one side of the issue.

William: Now, don't misunderstand me—I still don't believe my views on the subject are wrong. Whatever may be true of occasional figurative uses of the word, the accounts of immersion in the New Testament, and the fact that baptism is called a burial, are enough to settle the question with me.

Pastor Cowan: We still need to consider those cases you refer to, as well as this claim you've made about burial. But one thing at a time: we haven't finished evaluating how the word is used in the passages that clearly indicate its meaning.

WILLIAM: You've convinced me that *báptizō* is sometimes used in a figurative sense; I don't think we need any more examples. Besides, I'm impatient to hear what you have to say about baptism as a burial.

PASTOR COWAN: Don't worry—we will set your mind at ease and cover all of that in due time. As far as the use of the word, you're right that one example is probably enough. But I want to make it clear that we aren't limited to one single passage to help us understand the meaning of the word.

In Mark 10:38, while answering the request of two of his disciples to sit beside him in his kingdom—one on his right and the other on his left—Jesus asked them, "Are you able to drink the cup that I drink, or to be baptized with the baptism with which I am baptized?" And when they said they were, he promised, "With the baptism with which I am baptized, you will be baptized" (v. 39).

WILLIAM: A figurative use of the word—just like "drink the cup that I drink," this is only a word picture.

PASTOR COWAN: Very true, but it does help us to see how the gospel writers tended to use the word. What do you think Christ was referring to through his use of *baptism* here?

WILLIAM: Obviously his sufferings.

PASTOR COWAN: And would immersion make sense, in that case?

WILLIAM: Just a minute; I think you've made a mistake in your analogy here. I've heard the expression "immersed in trouble" plenty of times before. I think Jesus was referring to the troubles that had come upon him—he was overwhelmed with trouble.

PASTOR COWAN: I understand—you mean that, instead of coming upon him here and there in drops, trouble came in a shower or a flood?

WILLIAM: Yes, I'd say that's how the word is used.

PASTOR COWAN: Then what we are saying is even more similar than I thought. We don't disagree on the mode of baptism, but simply on the quantity of water to be used.

WILLIAM: I see you aren't letting go of my definition of *immersion*.

PASTOR COWAN: Well, regardless of that, at the beginning of our conversation we agreed that water was the element to be used, and I wanted to know whether you thought baptism depended on the amount of water or on how it was used. Would you like to change your answer now?

WILLIAM: Actually, I would prefer to move on to the significance of the ceremony itself and to hear what you have to say about baptism as a burial.

PASTOR COWAN: Since you seem so anxious to address that, let me warn you that if you still have any doubts about the meaning of *baptism*, you will have even more difficulty understanding its significance. Immersionists have always tended to interpret the passages where the word occurs by swinging back and forth from *action to quantity* and from *quantity to action* whenever it has suited them.

In the passages we have just considered, immersionists will often claim that what is occurring can be called immersion because it involves an *extra quantity of water* being used, but not because of any *action*. If they would keep to this, we might compromise and agree to the use of a greater quantity of water, enough to represent being enveloped. But no sooner do we try to make such a compromise than they tell us that immersion isn't a *quantity*, but an *action*; there must be a *putting down into* and a *taking up out of*—a burial. Please turn to another passage: Luke 11:38. Will you read it?

WILLIAM: "The Pharisee was astonished to see that he [Jesus] did not first wash before dinner."

PASTOR COWAN: The word used here is the same word, *báptizō*, that is used for the sacrament of baptism. What do you believe is meant in this context?

WILLIAM: I have to admit that immersion is not implied here—in fact, I believe in this case it would have been practically impossible.

PASTOR COWAN: Yes, it's common sense. First Corinthians 10:1–2 is helpful as well: "I want you to know, brothers, that our fathers were all under the cloud, and all passed through the sea, and all were baptized into Moses in the cloud and in the sea." Baptism is simply used to indicate consecration, and no evidence for immersion can be found.

Since you seem to be satisfied on the use of the word *báptizō*, we will move on to the issue you are most interested in: the significance of the ceremony. But I think it would be best to wait until another evening for that discussion.

6

THIRD EVENING, PART 1: BURIED WITH HIM IN BAPTISM

WILLIAM: If you are ready, I would like to discuss the symbolic nature of baptism. I feel more at home talking about the significance of the ordinance itself, and I'm confident I can defend the need for immersion against any arguments you may offer.

PASTOR COWAN: I'm glad you feel at home considering this subject—since you know what you believe, why don't you begin by telling me what you understand to be symbolized in baptism?

WILLIAM: I can give my explanation and the reasons for it in no time at all. I see baptism as commemorating the *burial* and *resurrection of Jesus*. Almost all the ceremonies instituted by God commemorate the times when he has interceded on behalf of his people throughout redemptive history. So, just as the Lord's Supper commemorates the *death* of our Lord Jesus Christ, baptism commemorates his burial and resurrection. I can't believe that God would be careful to commemorate all these other events and then fail to provide for this one.

It could be argued that the resurrection of Christ is the most significant event of all time. It's the basis of the Christian faith—the foundation of all our hopes. Without it, the whole structure of Christianity crumbles into nothing. It's such a huge, monumental event that it cannot go without being commemorated.

Through the eyes of faith we see Christ's broken body in the broken bread and his flowing blood in the flowing wine; shouldn't we also see his burial when someone is immersed and made legally dead to sin? And shouldn't we see Christ *risen* when the person is taken up out of the water after his baptism?

PASTOR COWAN: It's obvious that you are certainly at home with this subject and have given it careful attention. Your clear and thorough description of your beliefs has made me reconsider the order of some of the points we should discuss as we consider the subject of baptism. I agree with many of your statements—but may I ask what the *burial* of Jesus had to do with his work for us?

WILLIAM: I don't understand what you can possibly mean by that question! It sounds as though you believe his burial had nothing to do with his role as a Savior. Is that really what you mean?

PASTOR COWAN: It is. I'm at a loss to see how it serves any purpose in his work as a mediator. Let me ask what would have been different if, after dying at about the ninth hour on Friday, his body had been left on the cross until Sunday morning, and then he had come back to life and come down from the cross.

WILLIAM: Well, burial is a proof of death—it shows that the Savior was definitely dead.

PASTOR COWAN: Do you think his burial was essential to prove his death?

WILLIAM: No, I can't say that it was.

PASTOR COWAN: Then what do you say to my previous question?

WILLIAM: I suppose I don't see how it would have taken away from the saving value of his work. But his burial was intimately involved with his resurrection—and that, obviously, had plenty to do with his work.

PASTOR COWAN: Do you mean that the essential part of his resurrection was his coming out of the tomb?

WILLIAM: It was his coming back to life.

PASTOR COWAN: And he could have done that even if he had not been buried at all, couldn't he?

WILLIAM: I've never seen it presented in that light. But in any case, his resurrection was the most important event of all— even more so than his death. And since all great events should be commemorated, I believe that baptism should be used to commemorate the resurrection. Otherwise it would go without being commemorated at all.

PASTOR COWAN: I fully agree with you about the importance of the resurrection. His coming to life again, not simply coming out of the tomb, is the important thing. I also agree that such a great event should be commemorated. Let me ask you, though, on what day of the week was the Sabbath observed when Christ was on earth?

WILLIAM: I don't understand where this is going, but since you asked, the answer to your question is Saturday.

PASTOR COWAN: And now what day do Christians observe?

WILLIAM: We observe Sunday.

PASTOR COWAN: Why the change?

WILLIAM: Aha—I see your point. The change was made because Christ rose from the dead on Sunday.

PASTOR COWAN: Then the resurrection does *not* go without being commemorated.

WILLIAM: No, it does not. I never thought of it that way before, but it is actually commemorated better than any other event connected with his work.

PASTOR COWAN: Let me remind you of the two facts we've just explored: first, the burial of Jesus itself had nothing to do with his work in saving sinners; and second, we amply celebrate his resurrection by making Sunday, the first day of every week, our day to worship the risen Savior.

WILLIAM: But I'm not satisfied with the conclusion you've reached about the burial of Christ. You have argued that it had nothing to do with securing our salvation, and so you claim that it doesn't need to be commemorated. But I know this conclusion must be false, because Paul emphatically says, "We were buried therefore with him by baptism into death"—so baptism *must* symbolize the burial of Jesus.

PASTOR COWAN: I assume you're referring to Romans 6:2–4: "How can we who died to sin still live in it? Do you not know that all of us who have been baptized into Christ Jesus were baptized into his death? We were buried therefore with him by baptism into death, in order that, just as Christ was raised from the dead by the glory of the Father, we too might walk in newness of life."

WILLIAM: That's right—and nothing could be clearer than that.

PASTOR COWAN: Don't the facts that we just uncovered cast suspicion on your interpretation of this passage?

WILLIAM: If the meaning of the passage weren't already so clear, it might. But the language is so plain and straightforward that there can be no doubt about its meaning.

PASTOR COWAN: Perhaps, then, before we examine the passage, it may be helpful to look at its context. What is the first passage in the Bible that indicates to you that baptism refers to a burial, or specifically to Christ's burial?

WILLIAM: This one from Romans and a similar one in Colossians 2:12 are the only ones that teach it clearly: "Having been buried with him in baptism, in which you were also raised with him through faith in the powerful working of God, who raised him from the dead."

PASTOR COWAN: Is there any reference in the four Gospels or in the book of Acts that links baptism and burial?

WILLIAM: Nothing that I'm aware of.

PASTOR COWAN: And is Paul, in the sixth chapter of Romans, discussing baptism in an instructive manner? Does the context suggest that he is trying to *correct*, or *add to*, what he believes Christ and his apostles forgot to include in those earlier books on the subject of baptism and its role in the church?

WILLIAM: I can't see that he is. He refers to baptism because it illustrates a very important truth. It's a perfect example to illustrate our death to sin.

PASTOR COWAN: Let me ask you a question: What do you think of a denomination that bases its fundamental position on a passage of Scripture written thirty or forty years after Christ's ascension, when the writer had no intention to teach anything on the subject? Paul referred to it only incidentally, to illustrate a point that had no bearing on his main subject. And we could search through the four Gospels and Acts (or, for that matter, the whole Bible) and not find any other references that imply anything like what you're suggesting. Is this really a compelling argument for such a definite conclusion?

WILLIAM: In most cases I would agree that it's a little presumptuous. But if the reference is as clear as this one is, I think I have the right to call it an exception.

Rᴇᴠ Cᴏᴡᴀɴ: But suppose the passage had another interpretation, entirely different from the one you've given it?

Wɪʟʟɪᴀᴍ: Then the presumption would definitely be unfounded. But that isn't the case here.

Pᴀsᴛᴏʀ Cᴏᴡᴀɴ: A respectable portion of the Christian world says it does have another interpretation.

Wɪʟʟɪᴀᴍ: They are obviously mistaken.

Pᴀsᴛᴏʀ Cᴏᴡᴀɴ: I see you are not ready yet to examine the passage.

7

Third Evening, Part 2: Buried Together with Him into Death

Pastor Cowan: Let's step back and look at Christ's burial from a different standpoint.

William: I will agree to anything that will help us find the truth.

Pastor Cowan: A few questions, then: was Christ buried?

William: The Bible says so.

Pastor Cowan: Can you describe the circumstances of his burial?

William: Sure—he was taken down from the cross and put in a new tomb by Joseph of Arimathea.

Pastor Cowan: What was the tomb like?

William: It was carved out of rock.

Pastor Cowan: And what do the Scriptures say about the burial?

WILLIAM: His body was carefully laid in the tomb, and a stone was rolled against the door (Mark 15:46).

PASTOR COWAN: Would it have been substantially different if they had just taken the body to Joseph's house, put it in a small room, and then closed the door?

WILLIAM: It clearly says that the body was placed in a tomb—a sepulcher.

PASTOR COWAN: True—but was the action of doing this physically different from the example I posed? Was the body, when it was buried, *put down into the earth*, and when it was resurrected did it *come up out of the earth*?

WILLIAM: Let me hear your interpretation.

PASTOR COWAN: In a minute; let me ask you another question. Did the burial of Jesus bear any resemblance to a burial from today?

WILLIAM: Not much, no.

PASTOR COWAN: If Jesus' burial had been exactly like a burial today, would you maintain that immersion would be the proper way to symbolize it?

WILLIAM: It most certainly would.

PASTOR COWAN: Then does *immersion* mean applying enough water so that a person is hidden from view?

WILLIAM: Yes; so that the person is *covered*—out of sight and buried.

PASTOR COWAN: The *action*, then, is not important. Putting the person *down in* the water is not essential to immersion. It would be enough to *put* or *pour on* the water until the individual was covered.

WILLIAM: That could be considered a figurative immersion.

PASTOR COWAN: While still lacking the essential part?

WILLIAM: Paul says that baptism symbolizes the burial of Jesus, and that's enough for me.

PASTOR COWAN: Here is one more question, which I would like you to answer objectively and honestly. Forget about our modern method of burial, and consider only what the Gospels say about the body of Jesus after the crucifixion—that he was laid in a tomb cut out of solid rock. Now suppose this burial were to be symbolized with water; would immersing somebody symbolize the burial any better than sprinkling water on him?

WILLIAM: I don't see how sprinkling would symbolize it at all.

PASTOR COWAN: Not even figuratively?

WILLIAM: It would tax the imagination.

PASTOR COWAN: But you've said that enveloping someone would meet the requirements.

WILLIAM: Well, do you believe that sprinkling could symbolize Christ's burial?

PASTOR COWAN: Only by a drastic stretch of imagination.

WILLIAM: Then why are you asking me the question?

PASTOR COWAN: My real question is, does sprinkling symbolize burial any less than immersion does?

WILLIAM: To be honest, I don't see how either method does, without some definite creativity involved—but Paul says that baptism *does* symbolize burial.

PASTOR COWAN: That's the question we will now consider. What does the apostle want to communicate in Romans 6:2–4? What point is he trying to make? Baptism is introduced as an illustration, but can you tell me what is actually being illustrated?

WILLIAM: Paul has been saying that where sin increases, grace abounds all the more. This might seem to imply that since grace is greatest where sin is strongest, we should let sin continue so that grace may abound! To answer this ridiculous conclusion, Paul says, "By no means! How can we who died to sin still live in it?" Then he brings in the illustration: "Do you not know that all of us who have been baptized into Christ Jesus were baptized into his death?"

PASTOR COWAN: I see you have a clear understanding of the point he is illustrating. Baptism is introduced twice in this passage; will you repeat what is confirmed about it in both places?

WILLIAM: First, we are baptized into Christ; second, we are baptized into his death.

PASTOR COWAN: Very good. What do you understand by the first reference to baptism?

WILLIAM: Well, to get *into* Christ must mean to get into *union* with him, or, as we often say, to be "in Christ." So, to say that we are *baptized* into him means that baptism somehow secures this union.

PASTOR COWAN: You are an excellent theologian! Now what fact about baptism do you learn from the second reference?

WILLIAM: I suppose it means something similar. To be "baptized into his death" must mean to come into union with it. So just as Christ becomes ours through the first baptism, his death becomes ours through the second baptism.

PASTOR COWAN: Very good—and this is an important doctrine. In his role as Savior, Christ must be seen in all things as our *substitute*. His death was not, so to speak, a personal death—not simply the death of an individual named Christ Jesus. It was a representative death: he died representing us. Look on the cross and tell me who you truly see there, forsaken by God, suffering and dying?

WILLIAM: I see what you're saying. In the person of Jesus, our representative, we see God's people.

PASTOR COWAN: Then whose death was it?

WILLIAM: It was our death.

PASTOR COWAN: And how, according to Paul, does his death become our death?

WILLIAM: Through our union with him.

PASTOR COWAN: And how do we secure that union?

WILLIAM: Through baptism: being "baptized into Christ."

PASTOR COWAN: What verse comes after that?

WILLIAM: "We were buried therefore with him by baptism into death, in order that, just as Christ was raised from the dead by the glory of the Father, we too might walk in newness of life."

PASTOR COWAN: How does this verse tie the word *buried* into the overall topic?

WILLIAM: By saying *therefore*.

PASTOR COWAN: And what does that indicate?

WILLIAM: That it results from something in the previous statement.

PASTOR COWAN: What do you think is meant by "buried . . . with"?

WILLIAM: Well, I looked this up in a Greek New Testament and found no word that corresponds to our preposition *with*. Instead, one compound verb is used here, made up of two parts: a verb that means "to bury" and a prefix meaning "with" or "together with." *Buried with*, then, means "buried together with"; in other words, both burials (of Jesus and his people) were one—they were buried together.

PASTOR COWAN: To be "buried together with" certainly implies more than one person—you say the reference is to Christ and his people.

WILLIAM: That's what Paul says.

PASTOR COWAN: And how are we buried with him?

WILLIAM: The verse says "by baptism."

PASTOR COWAN: Look again.

WILLIAM: "By baptism into death."

PASTOR COWAN: And do you think this is equivalent to "by baptism into water"?

WILLIAM: I have always understood it to be.

PASTOR COWAN: But in the previous verse we heard the expression "baptized into his death," and you gave the only possible interpretation of it. And, as you acknowledged, this second statement is drawn from that; it alerts us with "therefore" that Paul is about to apply the previously-discovered fact here. In the first instance, "baptized into his death" meant to be so united to him that his death becomes ours. Here it must mean the same thing: that we are buried with him by being united to him.

WILLIAM: That sounds like a legitimate conclusion to me— the only possible interpretation, in fact.

PASTOR COWAN: But where do you see a reference to the *mode* of baptism?

WILLIAM: I've always thought it was there, but your detailed, step-by-step interpretation of the passage seems to bury it. I'll admit that I don't see it any longer. But doesn't Paul assign a special purpose to baptism? He seems to credit it with accomplishing more than either of us are admitting.

PASTOR COWAN: Not at all. As John says, "For there are three that testify: the Spirit and the water and the blood; and these three agree" (1 John 5:7–8). Something that's true of the thing a sign stands for can be, and often is, applied to the sign itself as being true by extension. Based on these statements from Paul, then, no one can draw the ridiculous conclusion that water baptism itself is what unites us to Christ!

WILLIAM: Then you don't think he is referring to water baptism here?

PASTOR COWAN: I don't think the mode of baptism was even in his mind. What he said would have applied just as well to any rite that represents what baptism signifies—our union with Christ.

WILLIAM: What do you mean?

PASTOR COWAN: Well, suppose that circumcision were still the rite of initiation into the church and signified our union with Christ. In this case the same language could have been used, but with the word *circumcision* substituted for the word *baptism*. Then Romans 6:3–4 would read, "Do you not know that all of us who have been *circumcised* into Christ Jesus [*united to Christ by circumcision*] were *circumcised* into his death? We were buried therefore with him by *circumcision* into death."

WILLIAM: I'm not in a position to argue with this theory, but I would like to know how another rite such as circumcision could symbolize the Spirit's work as well as baptism does.

PASTOR COWAN: Oh, there's no doubt that circumcision was intended to do exactly that. We often read of "circumcision of the heart." Paul certainly understood this symbol for the Spirit's work, because at the end of chapter 2 of the same book he writes, "For no one is a Jew who is merely one outwardly, nor is circumcision outward and physical. But a Jew is one inwardly, and circumcision is a matter of the heart, by the Spirit, not by the letter [written law]" (Rom. 2:28–29).

This shows that circumcision had the same significance as baptism—it represented the cleansing of the heart. And the same kind of substitution can be made in this passage, too—the word *baptism* for the word *circumcision*—and the symbolism remains unchanged: "Nor is *baptism* outward and physical. But . . . *baptism* is a matter of the heart, by the Spirit, not by the letter."

WILLIAM: I suppose I have nothing to say against your interpretation, but still, what you say only weakens my argument; it doesn't strengthen yours.

PASTOR COWAN: What makes you say that?

WILLIAM: Your interpretation would indicate that the significance of baptism throws no light on the mode of administering it. The definite examples of immersion in the New Testament, however, are still untouched and unanswerable.

PASTOR COWAN: That last claim remains to be seen. As far as the former, I think you're laboring under an incorrect view of the subject. I believe it can be proven, first of all, that baptism was not meant to symbolize or commemorate burial; second, that it was intended to symbolize the work of the Spirit; and third, that this symbolism does shed some light on the mode. The first point we have already considered—I hope to your satisfaction. But an exploration of the other two had better be saved for another evening.

8

FOURTH EVENING: THE WORK OF THE HOLY SPIRIT

WILLIAM: You've dismissed my view of the significance of baptism so handily that I'm anxious to hear what you have to say in favor of your own. It is always easier to put down than to build up.

PASTOR COWAN: Well, I can tell you that I won't base my view on a passage of Scripture from thirty or forty years after Christ's ascension, which refers to baptism only incidentally and only to illustrate a point that has little connection with it.

WILLIAM: That sounds fair, as long as you can deliver what you promise.

PASTOR COWAN: A few words, first, by way of introduction. Will you tell me how many members of the Godhead play a part in man's redemption?

WILLIAM: All of them. The Father sent the Son, the Son came and made atonement for sin, and the Holy Spirit applies the benefit of Christ's work.

PASTOR COWAN: Very good. Please name a few things that are included in the Spirit's work.

WILLIAM: Convicting us of sin, drawing us to turn to Jesus, and regenerating and sanctifying us.

PASTOR COWAN: Then he plays a very important part in our salvation.

WILLIAM: Yes—the biblical authors refer often to the Spirit's work.

PASTOR COWAN: Wouldn't you say that the Spirit's work is important enough to merit a ceremony that symbolizes it?

WILLIAM: I certainly would, and I've always thought that baptism fulfills this in some sense.

PASTOR COWAN: A very minor sense, according to your view, and only indirectly.

WILLIAM: Yes, our view is that baptism mainly symbolizes the burial of Christ. But I have often wondered, since the Lord's Supper refers exclusively to the work of Christ, why baptism does not refer exclusively to the work of the Holy Spirit.

PASTOR COWAN: It's a pity you didn't pursue your questions further; they might have led you to arrive at the whole truth. Let me ask you something: suppose you could find a place in the Bible where, for instance, John the Baptist had said, "Christ shall be buried in the earth, but you shall be buried by baptism in the water." How could I, as an opponent of immersion, explain away a statement like that?

WILLIAM: You couldn't—and I wish there *were* such a statement we could point to! It would settle the question and solve our discussion right here. But why did you ask me this? Nothing like that is recorded in the Bible.

PASTOR COWAN: I agree that such a statement would be conclusive, if we could find one; and I asked that question to lead into another. What would you say to a quote like this: "I have baptized you with water, but he will baptize you with the Holy Spirit" (Mark 1:8)?

WILLIAM: I recognize that wording from all four Gospels, and I admit it implies a close connection between the Spirit's work and water baptism.

PASTOR COWAN: So it does. The great work of the Spirit is to cleanse, purify, and sanctify. Should I quote some passages as proof?

WILLIAM: No, that isn't necessary. I know they are there.

PASTOR COWAN: And in a natural sense, water is a universal symbol for purifying and cleansing. The water of baptism in particular is described this way.

WILLIAM: Yes, I can think of passages that say this. Paul, for instance, was told, "Rise and be baptized and wash away your sins, calling on his name" (Acts 22:16).

PASTOR COWAN: These verses point clearly to the fact that using water in baptism commemorates or symbolizes the work of the Spirit.

WILLIAM: They do seem to teach this—but it's also frequently said that we are cleansed by Christ's *blood*. In 1 John it says, "The blood of Jesus his Son cleanses us from all sin" (1 John 1:7).

PASTOR COWAN: I'm grateful that you brought that up and quoted the verse you did; I was about to overlook it. Please read, in that same book, chapter 5, verses 7 through 8.

WILLIAM: "For there are three that testify: the Spirit and the water and the blood; and these three agree."

PASTOR COWAN: Please read that last phrase again.

WILLIAM: "And these three agree."

PASTOR COWAN: Do you see the connection between verse 8 here and verse 7 of chapter 1, where it says that "the *blood* of Jesus his Son cleanses [or purifies] us from all sin"?

WILLIAM: I do: both blood and water represent or symbolize the work of the Spirit. I agree with all this. But where does it lead us?

PASTOR COWAN: You will see soon. First we must examine a few passages that address the work of the Spirit. I will choose a few from the concordance and ask you to read them. Here's the first one: Isaiah 32:15.

WILLIAM: "Until the Spirit is *poured upon* us from on high."

PASTOR COWAN: Isaiah 44:3.

WILLIAM: "For I will *pour* water on the thirsty land, and streams on the dry ground; I will *pour* my Spirit upon your offspring, and my blessing on your descendants."

PASTOR COWAN: Ezekiel 39:29.

WILLIAM: "I will not hide my face anymore from them, when I *pour out* my Spirit upon the house of Israel, declares the Lord GOD."

PASTOR COWAN: Joel 2:28–29.

WILLIAM: "And it shall come to pass afterward, that I will *pour out* my Spirit on all flesh; your sons and your daughters shall prophesy, your old men shall dream dreams, and your young men shall see visions. Even on the male and female servants in those days I will *pour out* my Spirit."

PASTOR COWAN: John 1:33.

WILLIAM: "I myself did not know him, but he who sent me to baptize with water said to me, 'He on whom you see the Spirit *descend* and remain, this is he who *baptizes with the Holy Spirit.*'"

PASTOR COWAN: Mark 1:10.

WILLIAM: "And when he [Jesus] came up out of the water, immediately he [Jesus] saw the heavens being torn open and the Spirit *descending on* him like a dove."

PASTOR COWAN: Titus 3:5–6.

WILLIAM: "By the washing of regeneration and renewal of the Holy Spirit, whom he *poured out* on us richly through Jesus Christ our Savior."

PASTOR COWAN: And in Acts 2:17–21 the passage from Joel is quoted as having been fulfilled on the day of Pentecost. Keep this in mind while reading Acts 2:33.

WILLIAM: "Being therefore exalted at the right hand of God, and having received from the Father the promise of the Holy Spirit, he has *poured out* this that you yourselves are seeing and hearing."

PASTOR COWAN: Now tell me the different words that are used to describe the gift or the work of the Spirit in these passages.

WILLIAM: I can remember *baptized with, poured upon, poured out*, and *descending on*.

PASTOR COWAN: Do you recall any passages that represent the work of the Spirit as being anything like immersion?

WILLIAM: I was hoping you would ask that question, because there is a passage like that in the chapter we just quoted. It's Acts 2:2, where Luke is talking about the baptism of the Holy Spirit on the day of Pentecost. He says, "Suddenly there came from heaven a sound like a mighty rushing wind, and it filled the entire house where they were sitting." Here it is clearly stated that they were completely *enveloped* or, in other words, *buried*.

PASTOR COWAN: So, then, even though the Spirit was *poured on* them or *descended upon* them, as long as it was extensive enough to *envelop* them, it was still a baptism?

WILLIAM: In a figurative sense.

PASTOR COWAN: Well, I am both sorry and glad that you've quoted this passage: sorry that someone so intelligent would make such an oversight, but glad because plenty of others have done it before you, so we might as well address it. If you look at the passage, you'll notice that it says nothing about the Spirit himself filling the house. It was the *sound* that filled the house. Not until the third verse do we see a manifestation of the Spirit's baptism: "And divided tongues as of fire appeared to them and rested on each one of them."

WILLIAM: Now that I look at it again, I have to admit that I've never seen the passage in this light before. I've quoted it many other times before tonight and always seen it as an excellent example of figurative immersion.

PASTOR COWAN: Remember to keep in mind the key difference between us; you seem to want to ignore this difference when it suits your position. The whole question about the mode of baptism is this: Is the individual *put into* the element, or is the element *applied to* him? If enough water is applied to someone in order to envelop him, to call this baptism means deciding that the difference between our views is not based on the *action* or the *mode*, but simply on the *quantity*. If that is the case, sprinkling could meet your requirement as long as enough water is used. What do you think now—what was baptism meant to commemorate or symbolize?

WILLIAM: Definitely the work of the Spirit.

PASTOR COWAN: And what light does this throw on the question of the mode?

WILLIAM: I admit that it doesn't look good for immersion. It does seem to indicate that baptism involves *pouring* water *on* the individual. But this still means nothing for your side, since the cases of baptism recorded in the New Testament clearly point to the fact that immersion was the way used by the apostles.

PASTOR COWAN: We have yet to examine those passages; perhaps they aren't as decisive on the side of immersion as they seem to be from your standpoint.

WILLIAM: The facts and the circumstances around them are too clear to misunderstand. You couldn't succeed in convincing me otherwise without destroying my confidence in language itself! If something so clear could truly have an alternate meaning, I would have to conclude that nothing can be written plainly enough to avoid being twisted around to mean something different by somebody else.

PASTOR COWAN: Statements like that make it clear that your viewpoint is a lot more prejudiced than you think it is. You're claiming that all paedobaptists are either underhanded or foolish—that they either lack the common sense to see such obvious cases of immersion or lack the honesty to admit that they do.

WILLIAM: I'm sorry; I didn't mean to imply anything like that. But won't you admit that some cases of immersion are recorded in the New Testament?

PASTOR COWAN: The facts simply do not permit me to agree that immersion was ever recorded as having taken place.

WILLIAM: We would need a dozen evenings for you to try to convince me of something like that! But I am so interested in the claim you're making that I will come as many times as it takes to hear your arguments.

PASTOR COWAN: Actually, I think it should take only one more evening to say all that can be said on the cases of baptism recorded in the New Testament. Whenever it is convenient for you, I will be happy to address them.

9

FIFTH EVENING, PART 1: FULFILLING ALL RIGHTEOUSNESS

WILLIAM: I have read the stories of several baptisms now, and I think it's very clear that immersion was definitely the method used in each one. As long as we can take the language at face value, I think you are wasting my time. We have to conclude that John the Baptist immersed Jesus in the Jordan and that Philip immersed the eunuch.

PASTOR COWAN: Are these all the examples we can find in the New Testament?

WILLIAM: They are all I examined, and I believe they should be enough.

PASTOR COWAN: Well, before we go on to consider them, let's agree on how we will proceed.

WILLIAM: What do you mean?

PASTOR COWAN: We are going to examine these New Testament examples in order to understand what light they throw on the mode of baptism, correct?

WILLIAM: That is my understanding, yes.

Pastor Cowan: The evidence we will take into account is what is known as *probable* or *circumstantial* evidence. If we are going to examine these cases, it will be necessary to ignore every other kind of evidence. For the sake of argument, we will have to assume that all previous evidence we have gathered from the *meaning of the word* and the *significance of the mode* is equal on both sides. In other words, we will disregard any other kind of evidence about the mode of baptism except what we learn from the circumstances and facts of these cases.

William: That sounds fair to me.

Pastor Cowan: Then we are ready to proceed. We will first consider the cases you already mentioned.

William: Unless you have a strong preference, I would like to begin with John's immersion of Jesus in the Jordan.

Pastor Cowan: Perhaps it would be more accurate to say John's *baptism* of Jesus in the Jordan.

William: Either way; they both mean the same thing to me.

Pastor Cowan: May I begin by asking you why John baptized at all, and what characterized his baptism—in other words, what its purpose was?

William: John baptized because God sent him to, as John himself tells us. And regarding the purpose of his baptism, he said, "I baptize you with water for repentance" (Matt. 3:11).

Pastor Cowan: What does "for repentance" mean?

William: I would say it means he baptized the Jews to show them that they were sinful, needed to be cleansed, and should repent of their sins.

Pastor Cowan: Is this why he baptized Jesus?

William: Of course not! His baptism was different because Jesus was not a sinner. Jesus tells us why he was baptized: "For thus it is fitting for us to fulfill all righteousness" (Matt. 3:15).

78

PASTOR COWAN: What does he mean by "righteousness"?

WILLIAM: Actually, I feel particularly prepared to answer that question, because Dora and I have been reading through the first five chapters of Romans and have seen this word come up a lot. We are very interested in it, and I have been doing some study on the word. It's a legal term, which differs from *holiness*. *Holiness* has to do with our inward purity, while *righteousness* involves our relationship to the law—whether we've done what the law requires.

PASTOR COWAN: I'm impressed—I couldn't have interpreted the words better myself! It follows, then, that there must have been some *law* making it necessary for Christ to be baptized.

WILLIAM: It seems that way, from the language. I have never studied this myself, and I'm not as familiar with the Old Testament Scriptures.

PASTOR COWAN: The baptism of Jesus is interesting and important for many reasons, some of which are key to a clear understanding of our topic. Jesus is our Great High Priest; in fact, he's the only *real* Priest who was ever in the world. Aaron's priesthood was only a representation of Christ's, so Aaron and his descendants may be called representative priests, and Christ called the real Priest.

The Aaronic priesthood involved only the tribe of Levi, who were all descendants of Aaron. But as the writer of Hebrews says, "The one of whom these things are spoken [Jesus] belonged to another tribe, from which [tribe] no one has ever served at the altar. For it is evident that our Lord was descended from Judah, and in connection with that tribe Moses said nothing about priests" (Heb. 7:13–14). In verse 12, the author says, "For when there is a change in the priesthood, there is necessarily a change in the law as well."

Now when the priesthood of Aaron was first instituted, the tribe was formally consecrated to be set apart for their high calling. Whether every priest from then on was set apart this same way we don't know. But when a change took place as great as the one Hebrews speaks of, such as a change to *another tribe* (in connection with which, it reminds us, Moses said nothing about priests), then it would certainly be necessary for this new priest to comply with the law of consecration. It was *this* law that Jesus referred to when he said, "For thus it is fitting for us to fulfill all righteousness."

WILLIAM: That is very interesting and helpful. It does seem that Jesus was referring to that law with the language he used.

PASTOR COWAN: If we knew what this first method of consecration was for Aaron and his priests, we would also know what the second consecration looked like, in which Jesus conformed to the law and fulfilled all righteousness.

WILLIAM: It's too bad we don't have it recorded in more detail. That would have shed some light on the mode of Jesus' baptism and might have even settled the issue, preventing a great deal of arguing among God's people.

PASTOR COWAN: I appreciate your sentiment and agree—and I am happy to tell you that we *do* have this method of consecration specifically recorded in Scripture. Look at Numbers 8:5–7.

WILLIAM: "The LORD spoke to Moses, saying, 'Take the Levites from among the people of Israel and cleanse them. Thus you shall do to them to cleanse them: *sprinkle* the water of purification upon them.'"

PASTOR COWAN: *That* is the law that Christ said he must obey "to fulfill all righteousness."

WILLIAM: Are you *sure* he was referring to *that* law?

PASTOR COWAN: Yes. Let me list the reasons:

+ We know that there was some law he was required to comply with.

+ *Water* was definitely involved with this compliance.

+ And we have seen that he believed he must follow this law because he was about to enter his priestly work—not as a descendant of Aaron or of the tribe of Levi, but as a member of another tribe: Judah.

+ He definitely wanted to be baptized in order to comply with this law.

+ If the law of consecration is not the law Jesus was referring to, then there is no other law he *could* have meant, because no other law recorded in Scripture applies here the way that the law of consecration does.

+ And if no other law applied, there would have been no reason for Jesus to say that it was necessary for him to be baptized to comply with such a law.

William listened attentively to the pastor as he listed these six reasons. At last he spoke: "I admit that what you've said seems to prove that the law in Numbers is the same one Jesus referred to when he spoke to John."

10

FIFTH EVENING, PART 2: BAPTIZING WITH WATER

WILLIAM: There is one thing that still keeps me from believing that Jesus was fulfilling the law in Numbers that you claim he was.

PASTOR COWAN: What is that?

WILLIAM: The gospel record maintains that Jesus was *immersed,* not sprinkled.

PASTOR COWAN: That is speculation on your part; the Bible does not say that.

WILLIAM: In the first chapter of Mark it says, "In those days Jesus came from Nazareth of Galilee and was baptized by John in the Jordan. And when he came up out of the water, immediately he saw the heavens being torn open and the Spirit descending on him like a dove" (Mark 1:9–10).

PASTOR COWAN: Where do you see evidence for immersion?

WILLIAM: It says that he was baptized "in the Jordan" and he "came up out of the water."

PASTOR COWAN: Does it say that John put him *down into*, or *under* the water?

WILLIAM: Not exactly, but it does say that Jesus *went* down into the water, and "came up *out of*" it.

PASTOR COWAN: Didn't John do the same thing?

WILLIAM: Well, yes.

PASTOR COWAN: So was he immersed as well?

WILLIAM: No—but John didn't go into the water to be immersed.

PASTOR COWAN: But your only evidence that Jesus himself was immersed (which, you'll remember, must be circumstantial evidence) is that he did something that John did too.

WILLIAM: If John didn't immerse him, I don't know why he would take him into the water.

PASTOR COWAN: To baptize him, naturally.

WILLIAM: But the fact that he went into the water to be baptized shows that John immersed him.

PASTOR COWAN: Does everyone who goes *into* the water have to go *under* the water? I've seen plenty of people go into the water to refresh themselves or wash part of themselves off without actually going under it or immersing themselves. Even I, as a boy, would often go to the river for amusement, but since I wasn't there to clean myself, I would many times go *near* or *partially* under the water without completely immersing myself.

WILLIAM: If Jesus and John went into the water, though, they were at least partially immersed.

PASTOR COWAN: True—but is *that* what you insist on as your definition of *immersion*?

WILLIAM: Well, no . . . but I don't see why they would go *into the water* unless they were planning to be *immersed*.

PASTOR COWAN: And I don't see why they *should* be immersed just because they went into it.

WILLIAM: Then why would they go into it?

PASTOR COWAN: Well, certainly not to cleanse themselves in any literal sense. They went in to use water in some way to *represent* cleansing. Now, laying aside any preconceived notions about immersion, is it reasonable to take it for granted that Jesus was immersed?

WILLIAM: I always have. According to what you said yourself about the purpose of baptism (that it represents cleansing), this would certainly be best fulfilled by immersion. Immersion would represent *complete* cleansing.

PASTOR COWAN: I'm afraid you are taking that for granted also.

WILLIAM: I don't understand you. Laying aside *your* preconceived notions, wouldn't you admit that immersion represents complete cleansing better than simply applying a little bit of water?

PASTOR COWAN: That is a fair question; I will let God himself and Jesus answer it. Didn't God establish the consecration of the Levites in Numbers 8 to represent complete cleansing? And this purpose was fulfilled when only a small amount of water was sprinkled on the priests. Many other passages could be cited about ceremonial cleansing in the Old Testament, but instead I'll refer you to the language of Jesus in John 13:4–10.

WILLIAM: I can't seem to remember it. Would you remind me?

PASTOR COWAN: After observing the Supper, on the night of his betrayal, Jesus took a towel and "tied it around his waist. Then he poured water into a basin and began to wash the disciples' feet." When he came to Peter, Peter did not want him to go through with it. So Jesus said, "If I do not wash you, you have no share with me." Peter responded, "Lord, not my feet only but also my hands and my head!" But Jesus' reply was, "The one who has bathed does not need to wash, except for his feet, but is completely clean." Does this answer your question?

WILLIAM: It appears to; but I still don't understand why they would go to the river, where there was so much water, if they were not planning to be immersed.

PASTOR COWAN: If you think about it, it would have been strange if they had *not* gone to the river.

WILLIAM: Why?

PASTOR COWAN: The Bible tells us that multitudes of people flocked to John to be baptized by him. They saw him as the forerunner of the long-awaited—and now expected—Messiah. People from "Jerusalem and all Judea and all the region about the Jordan were going out to him, and they were baptized by him in the river Jordan, confessing their sins" (Matt. 3:5–6). Such large crowds wanting to be baptized would need water—not only for baptizing, but also to meet their own and their animals' needs. Therefore, no matter how much water was needed for their baptisms, they would still require access to a large supply of it, such as a river.

WILLIAM: So I'm assuming you believe that, even with the river there at their disposal, John did not immerse any of those who came to him.

PASTOR COWAN: Not only that, I don't think he would have done so even if anyone had wanted him to. Immersion would have failed to meet one great goal of his baptism. John said, "I have baptized you with water, but he [Jesus Christ] will baptize you with the Holy Spirit" (Mark 1:8). John saw his baptism as following the model of, or representing, the Spirit's baptism. And the Spirit *descended* on people; they weren't *dipped into* him.

WILLIAM: As you said, though, we are examining these baptisms based on circumstantial evidence, not based on the symbols they represent. Is there anything about the baptisms *themselves* that makes you think they were not immersions?

PASTOR COWAN: Oh, if I were on trial for my life based on circumstantial evidence half as clear, I would expect to be hanged! Look at it this way: John's ministry lasted about six months. From the passage we already quoted concerning the crowds who came to him during that time, we can estimate that he baptized about two or three hundred thousand people. That's an average of fifteen hundred per day.

WILLIAM: How could he baptize that many?

PASTOR COWAN: He couldn't—not if he did it by immersion. But he very easily could have performed that many baptisms with the method he obviously did use.

WILLIAM: What method was that?

PASTOR COWAN: The Bible doesn't tell us exactly, but we are safe in assuming that John's method of baptism would have been based on some corresponding ceremony in the Old Testament. Hebrews 9:19 will help to answer the question.

WILLIAM: "When every commandment of the law had been declared by Moses to all the people, he took the blood of calves and goats, with water and scarlet wool and hyssop, and sprinkled both the book [scroll] itself and all the people."

PASTOR COWAN: From this passage, as well as many similar ones in the Old Testament, it is clear that John probably baptized using a hyssop branch. This branch was particularly well-suited, and often used, for that purpose. Using Moses' method, John could have baptized thousands of people in a day without strenuous effort.

WILLIAM: And I assume you would say that's how the three thousand were baptized on the day of Pentecost, too?

PASTOR COWAN: Absolutely, though the circumstances were a bit different at Pentecost, since there was no river near where they were in Jerusalem. Remember, too, that the majority of Jewish people and leaders were enemies of the Christians. If the baptisms were done by immersion, there would have been at least two obstacles to overcome: first, finding a place that could accommodate so many immersions; and second, being allowed to perform them once this place had been found. These two logistical difficulties destroy the credibility of immersion. It would be hard to find a city anywhere in the world where so many immersions could have been performed.

It was nine o'clock in the morning when Peter began his sermon on the day of Pentecost. We don't know how long he preached, but we do have a portion of what he said: "And with many other words he bore witness and continued to exhort them, saying, 'Save yourselves from this crooked generation'" (Acts 2:40). The full account of the baptism is given next, in verse 41: "So those who received his word were baptized, and there were added that day about three thousand souls."

It would be a stretch to believe that so many people could be immersed in such a short time in a place like Jerusalem. On the other hand, these numbers make complete sense if the Old Testament method of baptism, given in Hebrews 9:19, was used. Two hours would have been enough time to get the water necessary for sprinkling and for the crowd to be baptized this way.

WILLIAM: I admit that the prospect of immersing three thousand people in one day has sometimes puzzled me. But I've seen calculations that prove it is possible.

PASTOR COWAN: Have you ever done these calculations yourself?

WILLIAM: No, I haven't.

PASTOR COWAN: Would you? I would like to hear them.

WILLIAM: Well, taking everything into consideration, I would say they might be able to get it all done in five hours.

PASTOR COWAN: That's a good start, but allow six just to be safe.

WILLIAM: There were twelve apostles, times six hours of baptizing for each, which works out to seventy-two hours of baptizing total. That means that each apostle would have had to perform forty-two baptisms per hour—about one immersion every ninety seconds.

PASTOR COWAN: Assuming, of course, that a supply of water was available and everything was ready beforehand. How likely does that strike you?

WILLIAM: Well, I'm inclined to think that each immersion would take closer to three minutes to perform with any sort of significance. But that would have taken more than twelve hours, not six. I guess I don't understand how it was possible in such a short time.

PASTOR COWAN: Judging from the *circumstantial evidence* alone, which position does the evidence support?

WILLIAM: Without taking into account the meaning of *baptism* or the significance of what it stands for, I have to admit that the circumstantial evidence of three thousand baptisms being performed in one day gives little support to the theory of immersion.

PASTOR COWAN: The example of Pentecost, though, was a digression. We were talking about the baptism of Jesus and of the crowds who came to John. Does the circumstantial evidence in *that* case support your theory of immersion for Jesus' baptism?

WILLIAM: If I concede the number of people who you claim John baptized, then immersion is definitely out of the question. But I don't believe there were actually as many as you say.

PASTOR COWAN: All right, then; I think two hundred thousand would be a fair estimate.

WILLIAM: That's much too high! Twenty percent of that sounds reasonable.

PASTOR COWAN: If you say so. That would bring the total down to forty thousand. In fact, let's divide it again by four, leaving us with only ten thousand. Now suppose that during his six months of ministry, John spent four days each week baptizing. In those hundred days, if he averaged a hundred immersions per day to reach our total of ten thousand, allowing three minutes for each immersion, he would have had to stand in the water for five hours each day. What do you think of the likelihood of that?

WILLIAM: I don't know what to say.

PASTOR COWAN: Do you think a normal person could endure that kind of exertion?

WILLIAM: It would be taxing, to say the least.

PASTOR COWAN: It's almost certain that no one could continue that kind of effort for such a long period of time. Even with a low estimate of the crowds who came to John, the circumstantial evidence does not bode well for immersion.

But to return to the case of Jesus, what would you say now?

WILLIAM: I'm honestly not sure. That was one of the strongest passages I had on my side. If we ignore the meaning of the word *baptism* and its symbolism as a burial, and decide based only on the circumstances, it does put me in a difficult position. The law that you say Jesus had to follow is a compelling argument. And the facts don't seem to present much circumstantial evidence that Jesus was immersed.

Pastor Cowan: I thought we would be able to get through the examples of baptisms in the New Testament in one evening, but it seems we will need more time. Think about what we have already discussed, and we'll return to this subject tomorrow night.

11

SIXTH EVENING, PART 1:
BAPTIZED AT ONCE

WILLIAM: I have another example of immersion, which I'm curious to know how you will try to explain away. It's in Acts 8:36–39: "As they were going along the road they came to some water, and the eunuch said, 'See, here is water! What prevents me from being baptized?'" After Philip explained to him the condition for being baptized, the passage says that the eunuch "commanded the chariot to stop, and they both went down into the water, Philip and the eunuch, and he baptized him."

PASTOR COWAN: And this strikes you as clear evidence of immersion?

WILLIAM: I have always thought so, yes.

PASTOR COWAN: Which part has the evidence?

WILLIAM: All the details of the baptism point to it. "They both went *down into* the water," and both "came *up out of* the water."

PASTOR COWAN: If these details prove that immersion took place, then both the eunuch and Philip must have been baptized, because the passage says exactly the same thing about both of them. Is immersion any more evident here than it was in the similar description of the baptism of Jesus?

WILLIAM: No, I suppose it's no different. But if you consider everything in context, it seems most likely that the eunuch was immersed.

PASTOR COWAN: What context do you mean?

WILLIAM: Both the meaning of the word *baptism* and the fact that they went into the water.

PASTOR COWAN: So you're taking it for granted that *baptism* means "immersion" and nothing else—which gives this story a context that, in turn, makes a case for immersion. You are making what logicians would call an *argumentum in circulo*. First you look at the word and say that it means "to immerse" because of the circumstances around it. Then you turn around and argue that the reason the circumstances point to immersion is because of the meaning of the word. That, I'm afraid, is circular reasoning.

WILLIAM: But it doesn't seem likely that this baptism was done in any way other than immersion.

PASTOR COWAN: On the contrary, everything points to a different method of baptism except for your bias that it must have been immersion.

WILLIAM: What do you mean by "everything"?

PASTOR COWAN: I mean all the *circumstantial evidence*. First, there is what we know of the geography. Gaza was some forty or fifty miles southwest of Jerusalem ("a desert place," v. 26), and from stories in the Old Testament we learn that it was a poorly watered area. Wells had to be dug to provide water for animals, and these wells were valuable property. We have accounts of wells like this in the story of Abraham (Gen. 21:25–31).

Remember that when Abraham's servant went to find a wife for Isaac, he stopped at a well where Rebekah came to get water (Gen. 24:10–21). In Genesis 26:12–22, Exodus 2:16–22, and many other places, we learn of the value of wells in that region. These facts about the qualities of the land in Bible times (as well as today) don't point to a good chance of finding enough water for immersion. (If by some chance there were a supply of water large enough, we would expect to see a settlement there that this passage could mention by name.)

Second, if we examine the passage, we see that the eunuch knew something about baptism already—believing it was his duty to be baptized. Philip, then, must have taught him something about it. Since they were looking together at the portion of Scripture that the eunuch had been reading before Philip arrived, the passage he was trying to understand must have referred to baptism. Let's look at it.

At the time that Philip found him, the eunuch was reading from the middle of Isaiah 53, which we learn from the quotation in Acts 8:32–33, and must have been studying it for some time. Now let's see if there is anything nearby in Isaiah (remember, at that time there were no chapters or verses in the Scriptures) that could have suggested to him the subject of baptism. Yes—earlier, in Isaiah 52:15, we find: "So shall he *sprinkle* many nations."

We learn in Acts 8:36, "As they were going along the road they came to some water, and the eunuch said, 'See, here is water! What prevents me from being baptized?'" It is obvious that the water he had read about in Isaiah not two minutes beforehand was still on the eunuch's mind when he saw this water. He must have already asked Philip what the prophet meant by saying that "many nations" should be *sprinkled*, giving Philip the opportunity to explain the importance of the *Spirit's work*, and how the water in baptism was the *symbol* of the Spirit's cleansing, *descending* or being *sprinkled on* those who trust in Jesus.

Third, from what we have already discussed about the surrounding area, it is logical to conclude that they must have come across only a small quantity of water. This is supported by the statement that they both went into it. Wearing sandals, they could walk into the shallow water without any real inconvenience, and Philip could take water in his hand to *sprinkle* on the eunuch, in keeping with the passage he had read—not to mention in keeping with the only scriptural mode of baptism.

There is also no hint of any preparation on their part for immersion—for instance, any dry clothing. If an immersion had taken place, we would expect important details like this to be mentioned, since Luke takes the time to record something much less important—that the eunuch "commanded the chariot to stop."

The passage ends by saying, "When they came up out of the water, the Spirit of the Lord carried Philip away, and the eunuch saw him no more, and went on his way rejoicing. But Philip found himself at Azotus" (vv. 39–40). We may conclude, then, that Philip's departure was sudden, that he was probably not able to change clothes, and that he most likely didn't travel twenty miles to Azotus dripping wet.

WILLIAM: All of this makes sense, but it's still just speculation. Is it right to draw these kinds of conclusions based on speculation?

PASTOR COWAN: Let me remind you that we are looking for probable or circumstantial evidence. As such, the best way to proceed is to formulate hypotheses and then see if the facts we know fit with them. Your hypothesis is that the eunuch was immersed, but all the probabilities point against it. My hypothesis is that he was sprinkled, and it seems to me that all the details support this conclusion. How does it seem to you?

WILLIAM: I admit that I don't see evidence of immersion here as clearly as I used to.

PASTOR COWAN: Do you have another case of New Testament baptism that you'd like to suggest?

WILLIAM: Nothing comes to mind.

PASTOR COWAN: Well, do you remember the baptism of Cornelius?

WILLIAM: Yes, I do, but I don't remember it saying much about the mode of baptism.

PASTOR COWAN: Have you ever checked the story to make sure?

WILLIAM: No—I can't say that I have.

PASTOR COWAN: Let's look at it for a moment, in Acts 10:44–48. At the end of that passage, we are told, "While Peter was still saying these things, the Holy Spirit *fell on* all who heard the word. And the believers from among the circumcised who had come with Peter were amazed, because the gift of the Holy Spirit was *poured out*, even on the Gentiles.... Then Peter declared, 'Can anyone withhold water for baptizing these people, who have received the Holy Spirit just as we have?' And he commanded them to be baptized in the name of Jesus Christ." May I ask you a few questions about this passage?

WILLIAM: Go ahead; I will do my best to answer them.

PASTOR COWAN: What was it that gave Peter the idea that Cornelius and his household ("his relatives and close friends," v. 24) should be baptized?

WILLIAM: The passage says it was because they received the Holy Spirit.

PASTOR COWAN: And how does it say they received the Holy Spirit?

WILLIAM: First it says that the Holy Spirit "fell on" them, and then it says he was "poured out" on them.

PASTOR COWAN: So Peter saw the Holy Spirit *falling* on them, or being *poured out* on them, which called to mind the need to baptize them with water. Would it be fair to say that when Peter saw that they were *baptized* with the Holy Spirit, he decided they should be *baptized* with water?

WILLIAM: I would say so.

PASTOR COWAN: Do these supporting details suggest anything as to how they were baptized?

WILLIAM: I guess they do, for someone who already believes in sprinkling.

PASTOR COWAN: Without corrupting the meaning of the passage, I believe we can make some changes to the wording that still preserve the main idea. The changes would look like this: "When Peter saw that the Holy Spirit was *poured out* on these Gentiles, then he saw that water baptism should be *poured out* on them." How, then, does Peter introduce the question of their baptism?

WILLIAM: By asking if anyone could withhold water from them.

PASTOR COWAN: Assuming that there was a place nearby where Peter was planning to immerse them, is this the most natural way he could have asked the question?

WILLIAM: Not really—I would have expected him to ask, "Can anyone prevent us from going to the water?"

PASTOR COWAN: What is the most obvious conclusion to draw from the wording he used—that they were to *go to* the water, or that it was to *be brought to* them?

WILLIAM: The second option seems more likely.

PASTOR COWAN: Now let's imagine someone who is completely unbiased about the modes of baptism. Which of these options do you think he would conclude had been used in this situation?

WILLIAM: The circumstances here, in and of themselves, seem to suggest that the Gentiles in this passage were sprinkled.

PASTOR COWAN: Can you think of another case of baptism in the New Testament?

WILLIAM: Nothing that would be of particular interest to us.

PASTOR COWAN: How about the baptism of Paul?

WILLIAM: Oh yes—now that you mention it, we do have that example.

PASTOR COWAN: Yes, we do—please read it, in Acts 9:18.

WILLIAM: "Immediately something like scales fell from his eyes, and he regained his sight. Then he rose and was baptized."

PASTOR COWAN: I would say the circumstantial evidence in this passage is especially in favor of sprinkling.

WILLIAM: I'm not sure I understand what you mean.

PASTOR COWAN: Do you know what Saul's physical condition was when Ananias visited him?

WILLIAM: Verse 9 of that chapter says that "for three days he was without sight, and neither ate nor drank."

PASTOR COWAN: And then what happened, according to verse 19?

WILLIAM: "And taking food, he was strengthened."

PASTOR COWAN: These verses indicate that he was experiencing great physical weakness, do they not?

WILLIAM: Yes, they do.

PASTOR COWAN: If Ananias were planning to immerse him, what would be a good time to do so?

WILLIAM: As soon as his strength would allow.

PASTOR COWAN: If it were up to you, would you have set him off on foot immediately to look for a place to immerse him, or would you have given him some food to strengthen him first?

WILLIAM: I would have fed him before making the trip, definitely.

PASTOR COWAN: And when did his baptism take place, relative to when he ate?

WILLIAM: It doesn't say.

PASTOR COWAN: Take a look at the eighteenth and nineteenth verses again.

WILLIAM: "Immediately something like scales fell from his eyes, and he regained his sight. Then he rose and was baptized; and taking food, he was strengthened." I see your point—he was baptized before he ate.

PASTOR COWAN: If you read this passage in the Greek New Testament, you will see even more clearly the circumstantial evidence against immersion. The word translated *rose* is a participle, meaning "rising" or "getting up"—a continuing motion. He could see again, and *rising up*, he was baptized. And after taking some food, he regained his strength. What do you think now about the circumstantial evidence around Paul's baptism?

WILLIAM: I understand how it could be used to strengthen your position on the mode of baptism.

PASTOR COWAN: Can you think of any other cases of baptism being performed?

WILLIAM: No. I think we've covered all of them.

12

SIXTH EVENING, PART 2: POURED OUT, POURED ON

PASTOR COWAN: I can think of another case of baptism that interests me, at least—the jailer at Philippi and his household, in Acts 8.

WILLIAM: I remember it now that you mention it. But I don't see how it helps us with the question of mode; the passage only says that the jailer "was baptized at once."

PASTOR COWAN: Remember, we are looking for circumstantial evidence. And I think a quick study will show us that this story is rich with it. We can find the account in the sixteenth chapter of Acts, but do you remember any of it already?

WILLIAM: I remember that Paul and Silas went to Philippi and, as a result of their preaching and a miracle done by Paul, they were seized and thrown in prison.

PASTOR COWAN: Do you remember the orders that the magistrates gave to the jailer?

WILLIAM: Let me look. . . . Yes, in verse 23 he was told to guard them carefully: "to keep them safely" and secure.

PASTOR COWAN: How did he carry out this order?

WILLIAM: "He put them into the inner prison and fastened their feet in the stocks."

PASTOR COWAN: What does this tell you about the layout of the prison?

WILLIAM: There must have been an outer section and an inner section—outer cells, I assume, for ordinary prisoners, and an inner cell to hold some prisoners more securely.

PASTOR COWAN: The Bible tells us there was an earthquake that shook open all the doors. When the jailer woke up and saw the prison doors all open, he was about to kill himself because he thought the prisoners had escaped. Does the passage tell us when this all happened?

WILLIAM: It says it occurred about midnight.

PASTOR COWAN: What did the jailer do when Paul shouted to assure him that the prisoners were all still there?

WILLIAM: He called for lights, rushed in, and fell trembling before Paul and Silas. Then he brought them out and asked, "Sirs, what must I do to be saved?"

PASTOR COWAN: Brought them out of what? Into what?

WILLIAM: Out of the inner prison, I suppose, and into the outer cells.

PASTOR COWAN: After Paul and Silas answered his question and told him what to do to be saved, what did he do?

WILLIAM: "He took them the same hour of the night and washed their wounds."

PASTOR COWAN: Then what happened?

WILLIAM: "And he [the jailer] was baptized at once, he and all his family."

PASTOR COWAN: When did the baptism take place?

WILLIAM: Between midnight and morning—maybe two o'clock.

PASTOR COWAN: And where did it take place?

WILLIAM: The passage doesn't tell us.

PASTOR COWAN: If it was done by immersion, do you think it would have happened in the prison?

WILLIAM: I've never heard of a jail that had facilities for anything like immersion! Especially in those days, when prisons were even less accommodating than they are today. But there was a river near Philippi.

PASTOR COWAN: So you don't think it was possible for him to be immersed in the jail?

WILLIAM: No, I don't see how it could have been done.

PASTOR COWAN: But they may have gone to the river instead?

WILLIAM: Yes, that's what they must have done.

PASTOR COWAN: And who was baptized?

WILLIAM: The jailer and all his family.

PASTOR COWAN: Did he have any children?

WILLIAM: It doesn't say.

PASTOR COWAN: If it had been only the jailer and his wife, wouldn't the passage have stated it that way?

WILLIAM: I suppose it would have simply said "the jailer and his wife." The wording does suggest that there were children.

PASTOR COWAN: So you think that the jailer locked the other prisoners back up, then he and his wife and his children went with Paul and Silas down to the river at two o'clock in the morning, were immersed, and then returned to the prison so the jailer could prepare a meal for the two disciples in his own quarters?

WILLIAM: It does seem strange that they wouldn't just wait until daylight. What was the hurry?

PASTOR COWAN: Wouldn't you call it unreasonable for Paul and Silas to take that man, his wife, and his children to the river in the middle of the night to immerse them? Not to mention requiring him to provide dry clothes for everyone?

WILLIAM: I agree that it sounds bizarre.

PASTOR COWAN: In light of the circumstantial evidence here, which method of baptism seems most likely?

WILLIAM: You've made a strong case; I can no longer see how immersion could have been possible in this instance. I had always just assumed that immersion was the only option; I never thought that such a strong case could be made against it.

PASTOR COWAN: And we haven't even seen the full extent of it yet! What did the magistrates do when it was daylight?

WILLIAM: They sent word to the jail to have Paul and Silas released.

PASTOR COWAN: Did Paul and Silas go?

WILLIAM: No, Paul refused to leave the prison until the magistrates themselves came and released them publicly.

PASTOR COWAN: Do you think Paul and Silas were honest men?

WILLIAM: Why do you ask that?

PASTOR COWAN: To help me make a point.

WILLIAM: Well, of course they were honest.

PASTOR COWAN: Then why would they refuse to leave the prison until the magistrates came, if they had already been outside it during the night *without* the magistrates' permission?

WILLIAM: That's a good point. I think we can be sure that they didn't leave the prison at all during the night.

PASTOR COWAN: I'm assuming it isn't necessary to ask you which view of baptism this case supports.

And now I think we are ready to summarize our investigation. Following our agreement, we have approached the subject by looking only at the Word of God. First, we have tried to find out the *meaning of the word* used to indicate baptism, *báptizō*. We looked only at the Bible because we wanted to know how its authors understood and used the word. We did not look at how other classical writers used it because the results would not have been relevant to interpreting the biblical text itself.

To discover the meaning of the word, we followed the same procedure used by lexicographers in order to find definitions: choosing passages where the word is used in contexts that shed light on its meaning. And as we did, we discovered that *báptizō* occurs nowhere in the Bible in a context indicating that it means "to immerse"—not a single passage can be cited. However, we learned that *báptizō* is used in several places to mean *applying water to something that is baptized.*

Second, we studied the *significance of the ceremony*, looking only at what baptism was meant to symbolize or commemorate. When we did this, we found that it was not tied to the idea of burial at all. Even if it were, immersion would not symbolize the treatment that Jesus' body received any better than sprinkling would. Jesus' burial had nothing to do with his work as Redeemer; he would have completed that work even if he hadn't been buried at all. And his resurrection, which immersionists are also inclined to tie to his burial, is already commemorated in full by celebrating the Christian Sabbath on Sunday.

We learned that baptism does symbolize *the work of the Holy Spirit*. "The *Spirit* and the *water* and the *blood*; and these three agree" (1 John 5:8). We found no examples where anyone was immersed in the Spirit; on the other hand, the Spirit is spoken of as *poured out on* us, *poured on* us, *descending on* us, and *falling on* us. So we reached the conclusion that in order to represent the Spirit's work, water must be *applied to* a person.

Third, we looked finally at all the examples of baptism in the New Testament that would throw light on the *mode*. We studied the circumstances surrounding the baptism of the crowds by John the Baptist, along with the baptisms of Jesus, of the three thousand at Pentecost, of the eunuch, of Cornelius, of Paul, and of the Philippian jailer and his household. We examined all of these cases for circumstantial evidence, and in every one the evidence was conclusively *against immersion* and *for the application of water* to those who were baptized.

These three methods of investigation were carried out independently of one another. Reaching a conclusion through any of them would have been enough, but for the sake of consistency, both in our findings and in terms of the Bible itself, it was best for them to agree with one another. And sure enough, each method led us to the same conclusion.

There is no need for me to ask you what decision you have reached, since the concessions you have made clearly speak for themselves. But now I suggest that you go to Pastor Roberts and ask him to go over the subject with you in the same way. Let him give you the meaning of the word first—I'm sure he will tell you that it means only "to immerse." Ask him for proof of this, but limit the discussion to the Bible, for all the reasons we've already mentioned.

Next look at the significance of baptism and ask Pastor Roberts for the biblical authority behind his assumption that baptism has anything to do with burial. When he quotes the sixth chapter of Romans, as I'm sure he will, ask him for a detailed interpretation of the passage. Then look with him at all the biblical cases of baptism in light of circumstantial evidence. In the baptism of Jesus, ask him to explain the statement, "It is fitting for us to fulfill all righteousness" (Matt. 3:15).

Remember: make sure that throughout this whole discussion, Pastor Roberts uses only the Bible. After investigating it with him, you can make a final decision—one that has been guided solely by the truth as revealed in the Bible.

But I would like you to come back for one last evening so that I can give you a general overview of the subject. Along with what we've already learned, this will help you to come to a clear understanding of baptism.

William thanked Pastor Cowan for his time and assured him that he intended to study the subject once more with Pastor Roberts. He left Pastor Cowan's home with an entirely new take on the issue—one that was completely at odds with his past beliefs.

13

SEVENTH EVENING: SIMPLICITY OF SERVICE

WILLIAM: I want you to know that after my last visit, I couldn't fall asleep until four o'clock in the morning! Even though I went to bed at midnight, I lay there the whole time thinking about baptism. I was determined not to let the conversations we'd had change my views, but I reviewed all of them in my mind anyway. I thought back to the meaning of *báptizō* as it's used in the Bible and remembered the passages you had quoted, but I couldn't find evidence for immersion in any of them.

I also revisited the significance of baptism. My position has always been that it commemorates Christ's burial, but no matter how hard I tried, I couldn't come up with any support for that view. In fact, the more I thought about it, the more I was amazed that I had never realized all these years how much better baptism symbolizes the *cleansing of the Spirit*. I suppose you could say that this "buried" the burial theory—so deeply that I couldn't see any trace of it anymore!

Then I reviewed all the instances of actual baptisms recorded in the New Testament. John's baptism of Jesus and Philip's baptism of the eunuch—examples that I once thought were definite proofs of immersion—seemed different to me now. The old certainties were no longer there.

I could picture John the Baptist, waist-deep in the water, immersing the crowds who came to him. I imagined myself trying to persuade him to stand firm and continue on with his work, but he gave me an astonished, pleading look, as if he were asking me, "Do you think I am superhuman, to be able to stand in this water all the time it would take to *immerse* the thousands of people coming to me for baptism?"

Then I saw him again, wearing sandals as he stood in the Jordan, and with a hyssop branch in his hand as he called those around him to repent. As they came to him, he baptized them for the repentance of their sins. He dipped the branch in the Jordan, and with one motion of his hand, water sprayed gently on the people and his work was done.

I tried to think of the baptism of Cornelius, of Paul, of the jailer at Philippi and his household—but all I could picture were images of water being *poured on them*.

The next evening I went to see Pastor Roberts. He had heard about my conversations with you and wanted to know how my study of baptism was coming along. I told him that it had put me in a very difficult position, and when he asked me why, I said I had encountered a new and different set of ideas—ideas that I had no way to answer. I asked him if he would go over the whole subject with me, the way you had. He agreed, promising me that one evening would be enough, and said he could provide any number of Greek lexicons to convince me that the word *báptizō* means "to immerse."

He suggested that I start by reading a book by a professor named Moses Stuart,[1] an academic who was a paedobaptist. He assured me that once I read the confessions Professor Stuart had made that went against his own views on baptism, I would be satisfied. I responded that I didn't care what anyone else had admitted about baptism: I was interested in what the Bible said! Then he said that he didn't see how it would be enough to settle the issue just by looking at the Bible alone! That was very surprising, after all I had heard from him and from others holding his view, claiming that they had the Bible on their side!

PASTOR COWAN: I'm glad that you visited Pastor Roberts, but sorry that he didn't agree to discuss the subject on your terms. I imagine he would have been satisfied to leave it with referring you to some Greek lexicons as his authorities on the meaning of *báptizō*.

If you'd like to explore the subject beyond what we've seen in the Bible, I would refer you to the work of Dr. James W. Dale on the classical use of *báptizō*.[2] Dr. Dale's book contains 670 pages of quotations from classical Greek writers, demonstrating that the word did not mean "to immerse."

As to the points that Professor Stuart conceded, I'm afraid they are not as persuasive as Baptists usually say they are. If they were, why didn't Professor Stuart change his own views and practice immersion himself?

1. *Is the Mode of Christian Baptism Prescribed in the New Testament?* (Andover: Flagg, Gould, and Newman, 1833).
2. *Classic Baptism: An Inquiry into the Meaning of the Word Báptizō, as Determined by the Usage of Classical Greek Writers* (Boston: Draper and Halliday, 1867).

But William, let me ask you this: where do you stand on the subject?

WILLIAM: I don't see now that there is any basis in God's Word for immersion.

PASTOR COWAN: I see.... Well, the last argument I was planning to introduce is a very strong one, even on its own apart from all the others we have seen. But since you are already satisfied, maybe it won't be necessary to explore it.

WILLIAM: No, please—I am interested to learn anything I can on the subject. I would be happy to hear what you have to say.

PASTOR COWAN: Well, I was going to suggest that we consider the question from what philosophers call an *a priori* standpoint.

WILLIAM: You mean one dealing with what we might expect or anticipate about things beforehand, based on the nature of how they are?

PASTOR COWAN: Yes—specifically, what we might anticipate from the New Testament *covenant* in contrast to the Old Testament *covenant*.

WILLIAM: I don't understand—how would this help us anticipate anything about baptism?

PASTOR COWAN: Can you tell me what God required from his people under the Old Testament covenant?

WILLIAM: The requirements in the Old Testament were often taxing. God's people had to perform many different rites, undergo ceremonial washing, and offer many sacrifices. This all took great effort and self-denial from the worshipers.

PASTOR COWAN: And what do you see when you compare the requirements of worship in the New Testament to the requirements from the Old Testament?

WILLIAM: A huge difference; the New Testament demands much simpler service from its believers and requires only a few sacraments.

PASTOR COWAN: Correct—there is a great difference between the two covenants. For instance, we could compare the Old Testament Feast of Passover with the Lord's Supper. These are good examples that nicely represent the differences between the two covenants. What can you remember about the Passover, as the Jews celebrated it before Jesus came?

WILLIAM: Well, it lasted for seven days, any kind of leaven was removed from their houses, and each household was responsible to provide a lamb that was slain on the first day, roasted, and eaten during the first night (Lev. 23:5–8; Deut. 16:1–8).

PASTOR COWAN: What can you say about the Lord's Supper, which replaces Passover in the New Testament?

WILLIAM: It is considerably simpler (Matt. 26:26–29; Mark 14:22–25; Luke 22:14–23; 1 Cor. 11:17–34).

PASTOR COWAN: As a rule, the structure of Judaism is significantly different from structure of worship in Christianity. Here is another example: What ceremony in the Old Testament made a man, outwardly, into a Jew?

WILLIAM: That's easy—circumcision.

PASTOR COWAN: Was this a simple ceremony?

WILLIAM: No; I'd say it was consistent with the complicated ceremonies we see elsewhere in the Old Testament.

PASTOR COWAN: And what is the ceremony today that makes us recognized, outwardly, as Christians?

WILLIAM: The one we've been talking about—oh, I think I understand where you're going. I can see the force of your argument.

PASTOR COWAN: Which would you say is simpler: circumcision, or sprinkling?

WILLIAM: Common sense would dictate that sprinkling is.

PASTOR COWAN: And based on what we have seen elsewhere, this is exactly what we would expect—for the New Testament rite to be simpler than the Old. Now, does immersion have this same simplicity?

WILLIAM: No, it doesn't—and I think I understand now. I'm surprised that it didn't occur to me before how consistent sprinkling really *is* with New Testament worship as a whole. In contrast, immersion is more of a throwback to the complexity of the Old Testament. It doesn't fit—it seems out of place in the New Testament.

PASTOR COWAN: I'm glad that you recognize the strength of our *a priori* argument. This is the same argument that first led me to question immersion, and to start looking to the Word of God for guidance in baptism.

Yes, I was almost as zealous as you are on the side of immersion when I was a young man. I remember I once went to a revival in Salem, Ohio, during the winter, where seventy people joined the Baptist church. One of the converts was my youngest sister, who was eighteen years old at the time.

It was bitterly cold outside and the ice on the nearest pond (which, I might add, was still a mile from the church) was twelve inches thick. I went to the "baptizing," as they called it, to see my sister get immersed. They made a large opening in the ice, and there, under those grueling circumstances, she was baptized.

This had a profound effect on my thinking. I decided that anyone who was willing to perform this duty under such trying conditions deserved great credit. And I think this same spirit of self-righteousness is one of the things that make immersion appeal to people the way it does. At least it was enough to satisfy my young mind at the time.

Later, however, I heard stories of immersions that were more and more complicated and required people to undergo more and more hardship to contend with their inconvenience—walking eight to ten miles in order to be immersed and so on. These stories made me start to wonder: Why should a ceremony that by nature seems much closer to the law of Moses, or even the Pharisees, be allowed to get in the way of the simplicity of worship in the New Testament church? This inspired me to examine the subject in the light of God's Word, and as a result I decided that immersion was not the method supported by the New Testament.

As a mode of baptism, I found immersion to be unscriptural. It failed to accomplish the purpose for which baptism was instituted in the first place: to *symbolize the gift of the Holy Spirit*. This process is best symbolized, as we have seen, by the *application of water*.

14

ADDING TO, OR TAKING FROM?

ABOUT TWO WEEKS AFTER William's final meeting with Pastor Cowan, the Presbyterian church had its regular monthly Communion. That morning William was received as a member and was baptized by sprinkling, symbolizing the cleansing of the Holy Spirit. Happy and content, William and Dora at last celebrated together the sacrificial love of Jesus, whose blood cleanses from all sin.

A few weeks later, William visited Pastor Cowan to tell him that he had been studying the foundational principles of the Presbyterian Church and was pleased with what he was learning. He was grateful, however, that those who applied to be members were neither required nor expected to agree with all of the church's doctrines. He said this was fortunate since he did not believe in infant baptism. He was glad that members were allowed to hold their own views on the subject—parents could present their children for baptism if they felt inclined, or they could let them reach a mature age and then decide the matter for themselves.

PASTOR COWAN: It is true what you say about the liberty we offer to potential members. We do not require our members to agree with all the doctrines in our confession of faith or our catechisms. Elders and deacons, when they are installed, are asked to consent to them, but people seeking to be members are expected to agree only on the major and most important doctrines of the church.

The specific issue that you mention, though, is one that I think some churches are guilty of ignoring and neglecting. I do believe that Christian parents who are members of our church have the duty to dedicate their children to God in baptism.

WILLIAM: What? I can't believe it—I thought it was understood that the choice was entirely up to the parents. It is not the church's business if some parents won't present their children. I have known many Presbyterians who didn't believe in infant baptism and didn't have their children baptized, and I've never heard of any of them being disciplined for this or accused of neglect. I even knew of an elder who never had any of his children baptized because he didn't believe in it.

PASTOR COWAN: Your last statement must be mistaken. Every elder, when he is installed, solemnly vows before God and the congregation that he agrees with the Word of God and all the doctrines found in our standards. I believe this is true of all Presbyterian churches; so if an elder were able to get away with neglecting this duty, it would be quite a surprise to me. I know that some members do neglect it, but I think churches that overlook this are wrong.

WILLIAM: So you would be in favor of disciplining parents for not doing something they honestly believed they shouldn't do?

PASTOR COWAN: No, not exactly—but I would reprimand them for not enjoying a privilege and not carrying out a duty clearly described in the Word of God.

WILLIAM: But suppose they don't see it as a privilege or a duty?

PASTOR COWAN: Then I would tell them to consult the Scriptures and learn about that duty.

WILLIAM: You may have convinced me about the right mode of baptism to use in general, but I still see infant baptism as an outdated Catholic relic with no authority from the Bible. You've had quite a time already talking me out of my support for immersion; but convincing me that it's my duty to baptize my babies—who don't even know what their own baptism signifies—would be even more difficult!

PASTOR COWAN: I haven't been aware of any real difficulty in our talks about baptism so far. All I've done is called your attention to a few facts in the Word of God. If you'll permit me to say so, it was your own bias toward immersion that was obscuring the issue and preventing you from accepting infant baptism.

Some people even try to combine immersion and infant baptism, but it's hard to condone that practice. When an adult, for example, is about to be immersed, the person overseeing the baptism can remove any possibility of unfortunate consequences by simply reminding him to hold his breath while under the water. But even these simple instructions would be lost on a baby, and a concern about the child's safety would unavoidably result.

I'm inclined to say, now that you have been set straight on the subject of immersion, that it will actually be easier to call your attention to a few passages in the Word of God that prove that infant baptism is a clear and enjoyable duty.

WILLIAM: I have to insist that that isn't true. I think the warning at the end of Revelation says it best: "I warn everyone who hears the words of the prophecy of this book: if anyone adds to them, God will add to him the plagues described in this book" (Rev. 22:18).

I won't settle for anything less than a positive command—a "the LORD God said." I have read the Bible from Matthew to Revelation, and I *know* there is no basis for baptizing infants!

PASTOR COWAN: While I don't agree with your conclusion on infant baptism, I do agree with the verse you quoted from Revelation. You didn't finish the quotation, though.

WILLIAM: I quoted everything that applied to us.

PASTOR COWAN: That is exactly the mistake that so many people make. Please finish reading it.

WILLIAM: "And if anyone takes away from the words of the book of this prophecy, God will take away his share in the tree of life and in the holy city, which are described in this book" (Rev. 22:19).

PASTOR COWAN: Both of these warnings are important to keep in mind. And while they refer specifically to the book of Revelation, I agree with you that they apply to all of God's Word as well. Immersionists accuse us of *adding* to God's Word, and we confidently charge them with *taking away* from it.

WILLIAM: But that doesn't change my point: anything that is important enough to be a matter of conscience must have a positive command behind it. The Catholic church claims to be able to dictate matters of conscience apart from the Bible's authority and to add to its commands and guidelines—through things exactly like infant baptism. But I maintain that the church has no such power; unless we have a positive command from Scripture, we are adding to the words of the Bible, just as Revelation says.

PASTOR COWAN: I would like to present two facts to you. You will not agree with them now, but I intend to convince you of them before we are done. The first is that those who oppose infant baptism are actually the ones who make inferences about God's law without having a positive command. And second, paedobaptists do have a positive command—a "the LORD God said"—behind our custom of baptizing our children.

WILLIAM: I think it will be hard for you to support either of those things, but feel free to go ahead and try.

PASTOR COWAN: I will proceed to prove my first point. Do you think the church has the authority to change the day we celebrate the Christian Sabbath?

WILLIAM: No, I don't—not even if the whole church were to agree on it.

PASTOR COWAN: I would say so too. But if the Bible gave us enough clues to draw an inference about it, would you agree that the change could be made then?

WILLIAM: Not just based on an inference—there would have to be a clear command.

PASTOR COWAN: What authorized the change in the day of worship from Saturday to Sunday in the first place?

WILLIAM: I don't remember, but I assume it was a positive, clear command.

PASTOR COWAN: Let me show you the two or three passages that give us the scriptural authority for this change. One is John 20:19: "On the evening of that day, the first day of the week," in other words, the same day Christ arose, "the doors being locked where the disciples were for fear of the Jews, Jesus came and stood among them." And then verse 26: "Eight days later, his disciples were inside again." And finally, 1 Corinthians 16:2: "On the first day of every week, each of you is to put something aside and store it up." Now, do you see any positive commands to change the day in any of these passages?

WILLIAM: No, nothing even comes close.

PASTOR COWAN: Yet these are the verses that give us the authority to change the day to Sunday. They show us that Jesus rose from the dead on the first day of the week and that the early Christians worshiped on the first day of the week. So I ask you: is there a positive command for this change, or do we get it merely from inference?

WILLIAM: And there's no better authority for making the change?

PASTOR COWAN: No—that's the best one.

WILLIAM: Then you are right; it's only by inference after all.

PASTOR COWAN: And to be consistent, if immersionists say that we must have a "the LORD God said" command for infant baptism, they should also be suspicious of Sunday as the day of worship.

WILLIAM: Yes—either they should be satisfied working from clear inferences or they should change the day of worship back to Saturday.

PASTOR COWAN: Immersionists maintain that their practices must have a clear positive command behind them, but here is our clear positive command for the day of worship: "Remember the Sabbath day, to keep it holy. . . . The seventh day is a Sabbath to the LORD your God" (Ex. 20:8, 10). We have no positive command, or "the LORD God said," that justifies the change to the first day of the week. Either we should change it back to Saturday, or we should all admit that arguments by inference have authority as well.

WILLIAM: I suppose, then, that your argument for infant baptism comes from inference too? Is it at least as clear as this inference for changing the Sabbath?

PASTOR COWAN: Oh, the argument for infant baptism is not at all inferential. It is a "positive command," a "the LORD God said"! In some ways the authority for it comes from inference, but even that inference is much stronger than any evidence we have for the Sabbath, which seems to have already satisfied immersionists.

WILLIAM: It's news to me that you can show me a positive "the LORD God said" command. If you can do this you will convince me.

PASTOR COWAN: Since you're a lawyer, you will appreciate the thrust of my argument. Tell me, once a law is put in place, how binding is it? How long does its authority last?

WILLIAM: A law is binding from the time it's passed until its obligation is satisfied, or until the law is repealed.

PASTOR COWAN: Can you tell me how this applies to God's law?

WILLIAM: Jesus himself answers this question in the Sermon on the Mount. He says, "Do not think that I have come to abolish the Law or the Prophets; I have not come to abolish them but to fulfill them. For truly, I say to you, until heaven and earth pass away, not an iota, not a dot, will pass from the Law until all is accomplished" (Matt. 5:17–18).

PASTOR COWAN: Can you tell me what law he was referring to when he said that?

WILLIAM: Are you asking whether he meant the ceremonial law or the moral law?

PASTOR COWAN: Yes.

WILLIAM: Both, I suppose.

PASTOR COWAN: What does he mean by saying that the smallest letter and the slightest stroke of the pen will not disappear?

WILLIAM: He means that the law will not be repealed or voided, or become no longer binding, in the smallest degree.

PASTOR COWAN: What does he mean by saying "until all is accomplished"?

WILLIAM: That the law will only be finished when all its commands are carried out and completed.

PASTOR COWAN: Would you say it's no longer necessary to follow a law once the reason that the law was laid down has been fulfilled?

WILLIAM: I would say so, yes.

PASTOR COWAN: Can you give me an example of a law that was fulfilled like this and is no longer binding?

WILLIAM: Well, the law requiring sacrifices is no longer binding because Jesus fulfilled the need for that law. The Jews offered animals to God as sacrifices to pay for their sins, and these blood sacrifices represented Christ, who offered himself when the time was right as a sacrifice to God. Since these sacrifices were modeled after him as the Lamb of God, they were fulfilled when he offered himself as a sacrifice. When he shed his own blood, the sacrificial laws were fulfilled and were no longer binding. Their reason for existing had been met.

PASTOR COWAN: You understand and have interpreted this well. There's another interesting and enlightening example involving the temple, which we can see in Hebrews 9. The inner part of the temple, the Holy of Holies (or the Most Holy Place, v. 3), was separated from the outer Holy Place (v. 2) by a curtain or veil. No one could go into the Holy of Holies except the high priest, and even he could only go in once a year, on the great Day of Atonement. We are told that the "regulations for worship" (v. 1) made it clear "that the way into the holy places is not yet opened as long as the first section [of the temple] is still standing" (v. 8).

The writer of Hebrews then explains that this all pointed to Jesus and represented his work. Since Christ was "offered once to bear the sins of many" (v. 28), now "we have confidence to enter the holy places by the blood of Jesus, by the new and living way that he opened for us through the curtain, that is, through [by means of] his flesh [body]" (Heb. 10:19–20).

The law that required the veil was fulfilled, or completed, when Christ opened the way through the curtain itself. When he entered the supreme Holy Place that was heaven itself, there was no more need for the Holy of Holies or the veil. As a vivid illustration of this, we are told that at the moment Jesus cried out from the cross and gave up his spirit, "the curtain of the temple was torn in two, from top to bottom" (Matt. 27:51).

WILLIAM: All of this is clear and educational, but I don't see how it relates to infant baptism.

15

A POSITIVE COMMAND: KEEP MY COVENANT

PASTOR COWAN: We have been discussing the law and its fulfillment as a lead-in to "a positive command," a "the LORD God said," which you say you need in order to be convinced. Please read Genesis 17:9–11.

WILLIAM: "And God said to Abraham, 'As for you, you shall keep my covenant, you and your offspring after you throughout their generations. This is my covenant, which you shall keep, between me and you and your offspring after you: *Every male among you shall be circumcised. . . .* And it shall be a sign of the covenant between me and you.'"

PASTOR COWAN: Now here is a law decreed and set forth by God himself. It is a both a "positive command" and a "the LORD God said"! So here is the question: How long did this law apply?

WILLIAM: It must have applied to the covenant God is describing—the Old Testament covenant—and ended when it ended.

PASTOR COWAN: What makes you say that?

WILLIAM: Well, God made that covenant with Abraham and his offspring. The Israelites were his offspring, so it must have applied only to them.

PASTOR COWAN: Will you read Galatians 3:7?

WILLIAM: "Know then that it is those of faith who are the sons of Abraham."

PASTOR COWAN: And verse 29.

WILLIAM: "And if you are Christ's, then you are Abraham's offspring, heirs according to promise."

PASTOR COWAN: The covenant God made with Abraham was the covenant of grace: Abraham and his descendants would be saved by faith. And the passages you just read clearly show who the descendants of Abraham are. Scripture states that they were not only Abraham's physical offspring but, in fact, *all* people who embrace God by faith.

WILLIAM: But didn't the ceremonial law no longer apply once Christ came?

PASTOR COWAN: Keeping in mind the passage you quoted earlier from the Sermon on the Mount, about what is required for the law to pass away, what reason do you have to think that the ceremonial law does not apply?

WILLIAM: Well, Christ fulfilled it.

PASTOR COWAN: If it is true that Christ fulfilled this law, then it is certainly no longer binding. But now we have reached a turning point in our conversation. Up until now the burden of proof has been on me to come up with a positive command. Now that I have produced one, it falls to you to show that this command—the law requiring circumcision—is no longer binding.

You said yourself that a law is binding until it is either fulfilled or repealed; anyone else would say the same. And we have found one, set forth by God, that requires the seal of the covenant to be made to the children in Abraham's line—which is now anyone who is in Christ, the heirs of the promise (Gal. 3:17–18). With that my work is done, and now yours begins. It's up to you to prove that this law is no longer binding.

WILLIAM: Now I see where you've been leading me. I must admit, I've never heard this approach before, and it does sound compelling. But I think I can convince you that this law no longer applies.

PASTOR COWAN: And if you can't, then what?

WILLIAM: Then I'd have to say that the law is still as binding as when it was first given to Abraham. But I believe it has ended, along with all the other ceremonial laws of the Old Testament.

PASTOR COWAN: That is just an assumption—I demand a "the LORD God said"!

WILLIAM: Well, if you're going to insist on that, you might as well say that most of the other ceremonial laws still apply, too. Just because we don't have an instance of "the LORD God said" for each one doesn't mean that these laws haven't been repealed.

PASTOR COWAN: My demand is a reasonable and, in fact, a necessary one. You yourself gave us our principle that a law is binding until it is fulfilled or repealed. Now, we agree that any laws from the Old Testament that haven't been fulfilled or repealed are still binding, and the truth is, most of the ceremonial laws foreshadowed Christ and his work and were indeed fulfilled by him. Therefore it's true that they have ended.

The law that requires us to observe the Sabbath, however, did *not* relate to Christ or his work, and was not fulfilled by him. Therefore it is still binding. And the law requiring Abraham and his seed after him to apply the seal of the covenant to their infant children was also not related to Christ or his work, and was not fulfilled by Christ. It is an assumption to say that this law ceased just because the laws about sacrifices came to an end.

WILLIAM: I can see now the distinction you're making. And it does agree with the verse, "Until heaven and earth pass away, not an iota, not a dot, will pass from the Law until all is accomplished" (Matt. 5:18). I admit that this law about applying the seal of the covenant to Abraham's children was not fulfilled by Christ or his work.

PASTOR COWAN: Thank you for being willing to acknowledge an error when it is pointed out to you.

WILLIAM: But I'm confused. The law makes it clear that children should be circumcised, but circumcision, you will agree, has now ended. So on that basis alone, doesn't that mean that the law that required it is no longer binding?

PASTOR COWAN: Unfortunately you have given up one assumption and taken on another one. You're drawing a conclusion about the law based on the results that you see. But that is also an assumption. I maintain that the *law* requiring circumcision itself has *not* ceased to be binding, and if you want to convince me otherwise, I demand proof. I will be satisfied with nothing less than "the LORD God said."

WILLIAM: But it's true that the rite of circumcision has ended. Are you saying it hasn't?

PASTOR COWAN: No, I acknowledge that it has. But can you show me the authority for this?

WILLIAM: No, I can't. I only know that it stopped after the establishment of the New Testament church. Can you give me the specific reason?

PASTOR COWAN: Yes, I can.

WILLIAM: I would like to hear it.

PASTOR COWAN: This task really falls to those who oppose infant baptism, but they can never give a reason why we do not still circumcise children. They insist on *taking from* the Word of God based on mere assumption. In reality, circumcision was ended through the very same process that caused Passover to end—what we call *substitution*.

The law that we are looking at has two important aspects to consider: First, and most importantly, it required parents to consecrate their children to God by applying the seal of the covenant to them. And second, at the time it was given, the law specified that this seal should be circumcision.

The essential part of the law was the consecration itself—the applying of the seal. The rite, which was originally circumcision, could end if it were replaced with another rite, either of the same kind or for the same purpose. But the law itself, requiring children to be consecrated to God, stands to this day *unfulfilled* and *unrepealed*.

WILLIAM: I suppose you mean that infant baptism has taken its place? What authority do you have for saying that circumcision has been replaced like this by something else? How do you know that baptism has the same purpose—consecrating children to God?

PASTOR COWAN: Yes, I *do* mean that baptism has replaced circumcision. And the proof is very clear:

First, the two rites have the same purpose—and here, to answer your question, is how I know. Circumcision was the rite of initiation into the church under the old covenant. Through this rite, men became Jews. Baptism is the rite of initiation into the church under the new covenant. Through this rite we are recognized as members of God's family. They both have the purpose of initiation for members of God's people.

Second, they both have the same significance. Circumcision symbolized the purity of the heart. A few passages will confirm this:

- Deuteronomy 10:16: "Circumcise therefore the foreskin of your heart, and be no longer stubborn."
- Deuteronomy 30:6: "The LORD your God will circumcise your heart and the heart of your offspring, so that you will love the LORD your God with all your heart and with all your soul, that you may live."
- Jeremiah 4:4: "Circumcise yourselves to the LORD; remove the foreskin of your hearts, O men of Judah and inhabitants of Jerusalem."
- Romans 2:28–29: "For no one is a Jew who is merely one outwardly, nor is circumcision outward and physical. But a Jew is one inwardly, and circumcision is a matter of the heart, by the Spirit, not by the letter [written law]. His [the Jew's] praise is not from man but from God."

As we have already seen, baptism symbolizes the same thing. As John says, "For there are three that testify: the Spirit and the water and the blood; and these three agree" (1 John 5:7–8). Christ's blood cleanses us, and both the Spirit and the water symbolize this cleansing.

WILLIAM: But the Israelites had a unique situation: they were both a church and a state. Wasn't circumcision more of a national badge that indicated citizenship instead of church membership?

PASTOR COWAN: That is an old objection that opponents of infant baptism have always used to evade the truth. It is true that Israel was both a nation and a church. But it's also true that these two aspects formed one single *theocracy*. There were not two different groups in charge; to belong to the nation was to belong to the church and vice versa.

WILLIAM: But didn't circumcision relate more to the citizenship aspect than to membership in the church?

PASTOR COWAN: What I've said about the *significance* of circumcision should have already answered this question. But I'll cite another authority to show you the error of what you're suggesting. When I told you that circumcision was the *seal of the covenant of grace*, I expected you to ask for the authority behind that. So I will now show you how circumcision referred specifically to the church, instead of the nation, and how it was a seal of the covenant of grace. Please read the first part of Romans 4:11.

WILLIAM: "He received the sign of circumcision as a seal of the righteousness that he had by faith while he was still uncircumcised."

PASTOR COWAN: Who is this verse describing?

WILLIAM: Abraham.

PASTOR COWAN: And what is a seal?

WILLIAM: Something that's applied to an agreement or a contract, to formalize or confirm it.

PASTOR COWAN: What does the verse say that circumcision was given as a seal of?

WILLIAM: Righteousness.

PASTOR COWAN: So what does that indicate?

WILLIAM: "A seal of righteousness" is a confirmation that he was righteous.

PASTOR COWAN: How did Abraham become righteous?

WILLIAM: Through his faith.

PASTOR COWAN: Correct. We are taught that Abraham was justified *by faith*; God regarded him and treated him as righteous because of his faith. To confirm this, God gave him circumcision as a seal of the covenant of grace. We are clearly taught the *purpose* of circumcision here at its beginning: it was given to Abraham "as a seal of the righteousness that he had by faith while he was still uncircumcised." Does Paul's wording answer your question?

WILLIAM: I've never considered circumcision from that viewpoint before. Now I see, based on these verses, that circumcision was instituted to symbolize someone's connection to the church. It was a seal of the covenant of grace, and its purpose and significance were the same as those of baptism today.

PASTOR COWAN: That's right. The law requiring children to be consecrated to God has *not been repealed*. The rite has merely been changed—from circumcision to baptism. The New Testament rite is simpler, but its purpose and significance are the same. Is it clear now that the one takes the place of the other?

WILLIAM: It does seem that way—but there is a major difference between the two. Only male children were circumcised, and yet we baptize both sexes.

PASTOR COWAN: A good question, but not a very difficult one. It is true that the seal of circumcision applied only to males; it was not performed on females of any age. At that time women were included as members of the church because they were represented by the men. But in the New Testament church, women become members through their own profession of faith. The rite was changed to reflect this, and now women are included. We see this in the case of Lydia in Acts 16.

In the old covenant, female infants did not have the seal applied to them for the same reason female adults didn't. And now, since female adults have the new seal applied to them, it should also be applied to female infants. Wouldn't you say it is assumed that some of the New Testament households that were baptized included female children? No distinction was made or mentioned about the gender of the children in any of the households.

WILLIAM: I admit I didn't think it was much of an objection in the first place, but I thought I would mention it anyway, just to see how you would answer. You have certainly satisfied it.

16

Two Covenants, One Church

WILLIAM: It seems to me, throughout all the arguments you've made in our talks about the church, that you assume the *two covenants* (with some small, inconsequential changes) are really *only one*. Is this true?

PASTOR COWAN: It is true that I believe the two covenants encompass one church. But let me address your claim that I have made an assumption in thinking so—I believe it will be easy to show that what I am saying is the truth. I submit that the church, from the time it formally began under Abraham until the end of the world, is in all fundamental ways one and the same.

In the process of arguing this proposal, I will also demonstrate that our obligation to dedicate our children to God continues to this day. It is a law given to God's people that has not been repealed, and if God's people are the same today as they were when it was given, the conclusion is only logical.

WILLIAM: This sounds like a difficult task you've undertaken. How can you say that the Israelites were in any way the same as the Christian church?

PASTOR COWAN: I think we will find it very easy to support this, because of how much evidence we will find in the Word of God. William, what would you say is the primary, central foundation of the church? Who makes the church possible?

WILLIAM: Jesus, our Savior. The Son of God and Son of Man who died for sinners.

PASTOR COWAN: So he is our Savior?

WILLIAM: Yes—our only Savior.

PASTOR COWAN: And did Abraham, David, and Isaiah have a Savior?

WILLIAM: Yes, I suppose they did.

PASTOR COWAN: Who was their Savior?

WILLIAM: Well, there never was and never could be anyone other than Jesus.

PASTOR COWAN: Very good. Jesus himself said, "Abraham rejoiced that he would see my day. He saw it and was glad" (John 8:56). The Bible teaches us that there can be no salvation without a Savior. Jesus is the only one who could fulfill the requirements of this Savior, so both covenants had him as their Savior. Tell me, then, what is essential for salvation? How are we saved?

WILLIAM: By faith in the Lord Jesus.

PASTOR COWAN: And how were the Jewish people saved in the Old Testament?

WILLIAM: The Bible says that Abraham was justified by faith.

PASTOR COWAN: In Romans 4, Paul points to Abraham as an example to demonstrate that we too are justified by faith. After showing that Abraham's faith was "counted to him as righteousness" (Rom. 4:22), Paul concludes the chapter this way: "The words 'it was counted to him' were not written for his sake alone, but for ours also. It will be counted to us who believe in him who raised from the dead Jesus our Lord" (v. 23–24). Both the *Savior* and the *plan of salvation* were identical under both covenants. This is an important fact.

WILLIAM: Yes, I can see that they are both the same.

PASTOR COWAN: Now, the church is the body of believers— those who receive the Lord Jesus as their Savior. The way that they confess him as their Savior may have changed, following the will of God, but the essential parts remain the same. Once circumcision was the seal of the covenant; now, by the authority of God, it is baptism. Opponents of infant baptism draw a very clear distinction between the two covenants. Sometimes they even give the impression that the gospel is only for us.

WILLIAM: I thought it was.

PASTOR COWAN: The gospel is the good news of salvation through Jesus; but this good news also came to the Jews in the Old Testament. Scripture says, "For good news came to us just as to them" (Heb. 4:2). "Them" means those living under the old covenant; the gospel was preached to them just as it was to us. They looked forward to, and trusted in, the coming Savior.

Paul often speaks of the characteristics of the church under both covenants. In Romans 11 he describes the church as a tree: The Israelites under the old covenant, and the Gentiles under the new, are the branches. The Israelites are the natural branches, and the Gentiles are shoots from another tree that have been grafted in with them:

> But if some of the branches were broken off, and you, although a wild olive shoot, were grafted in among the others and now share in

the nourishing root of the olive tree, do not be arrogant toward the branches. If you are, remember it is not you who support the root, but the root that supports you. Then you will say, "Branches were broken off so that I might be grafted in." That is true. They were broken off because of their unbelief, but you stand fast through faith. So do not become proud, but fear. For if God did not spare the natural branches, neither will he spare you (Rom. 11:17–21).

It is difficult to understand how anyone could read something like this and not see the church as *one and the same* under both covenants.

Paul also wrote to Timothy, urging him to "continue in what you have learned and have firmly believed." He reminded him "how from childhood you have been acquainted with the sacred writings, which are able to make you wise for salvation through faith in Christ Jesus" (2 Tim. 3:14–15).

When Timothy was a child, the only Scriptures he had were the Old Testament. In the next verse (v. 16), Paul says these same Scriptures are *profitable* for all things, and he has already said in verse 15 that they are able to make us "wise for salvation." How? The same way that the New Testament makes us wise for salvation: "through faith in Christ Jesus."

Now tell me—have I sufficiently proved that the church is the same under both covenants?

WILLIAM: So in your view, the Jewish church from the Old Testament has just as much right to be called *Christian* as the church of today?

PASTOR COWAN: Why is today's church called the Christian church?

WILLIAM: Because Christ is the Head of the church and its Savior.

PASTOR COWAN: And who was the Head and Savior of the Jewish church?

WILLIAM: Christ was.

PASTOR COWAN: Then wasn't it as much the Christian church as the church is today?

WILLIAM: I guess I don't see why not.

PASTOR COWAN: Don't forget the question underlying all of this. In the church under the old covenant of Abraham, God gave parents a command to consecrate their children to him. This law has not been fulfilled or repealed; nothing has put an end to it. So is it still binding?

WILLIAM: But I don't see the good of baptizing an infant who doesn't even know what is happening.

PASTOR COWAN: I'll set aside for now the question I asked, which you have not yet answered, and address this new point you have raised. Let me ask what the "good" is of baptizing anyone.

WILLIAM: Well, it's a duty required by Jesus.

PASTOR COWAN: Yes—as is the baptism of infants. But by the same token, what was the "good" of circumcising infants who didn't know what circumcision meant?

WILLIAM: But we are told to repent and believe, and *then* be baptized. Infants cannot repent or believe, so they can't be baptized.

PASTOR COWAN: But we can't be saved unless we repent and believe, either: "Whoever does not believe is condemned already" (John 3:18). Are you saying that because infants can't believe, they cannot be saved?

WILLIAM: Well, no—the command to repent and believe applies only to adults: those who already can believe.

PASTOR COWAN: What reason do you have for thinking that the command has those limitations? I don't see anything like that even implied in the context.

WILLIAM: Well, it goes without saying. The very nature of things demands it. Without a limitation like that, we would have to conclude that any infants who die are lost. Don't you believe they are saved?

PASTOR COWAN: Yes, I believe any covenant babies who die are saved.

WILLIAM: Then passages like these cannot refer to infants.

PASTOR COWAN: I agree that you're right—my only objection is that you apply that line of reasoning when it suits your purpose, and then disregard it when it suits a different purpose.

WILLIAM: What do you mean?

PASTOR COWAN: When repentance and faith are given as requirements for baptism, you make a case against infant baptism because infants can't believe—assuming that these requirements apply to anyone who is to be baptized. But when the question of babies dying in infancy comes up, you say the passages apply only to adults who can believe. Which is it?

WILLIAM: I admit that I see why you are criticizing my approach. I never realized before how I was changing my line of thought to suit my argument. But I still say it's unreasonable to perform baptism on an infant who knows nothing about its meaning or significance.

PASTOR COWAN: I'm assuming that your emotions are aroused at the thought of an infant being baptized. You think, *How can parents like that be so superstitious, and* add to *the commands God has given us?*

WILLIAM: Yes, that's an accurate description of my feelings about babies being baptized.

PASTOR COWAN: It's sad that opponents of infant baptism have so little regard for the Old Testament and take comfort in seeing it as obsolete and unnecessary.

WILLIAM: Why do you say that?

PASTOR COWAN: Because if they took the Old Testament seriously, they would have the same qualms about infants being circumcised at only eight days old—infants who knew "nothing about its meaning or significance." This meaning and significance, as we have seen, was the same for circumcision as it was for baptism. So the same objections should be made against the one as against the other. But I guess you would excuse those ancient Israelites for such foolish superstitions, because of the uncivilized age they lived in.

WILLIAM: But circumcision was required by God himself!

PASTOR COWAN: Exactly! I wish you would be honest enough to consider whether the objections you raise against infant baptism couldn't apply just as well to circumcision.

WILLIAM: Maybe you are right.

17

Children of the Covenant

WILLIAM: Even if I agree, however, that the promise and the law given to Abraham were *not* repealed, isn't it strange that there is no indication in the New Testament that they still apply?

PASTOR COWAN: Before I answer that question, let me ask you another one. If it were true that this promise was still binding, what evidence would you expect to find of this?

WILLIAM: I would expect to find statements in the Bible confirming that it still applies to us, or demonstrating that it is still required.

PASTOR COWAN: Which is exactly what we find in the New Testament! On the day of Pentecost, when the crowds asked, "Brothers, what shall we do?" (Acts 2:37), Peter told them first that they must "repent and be baptized" (v. 38). Then he said, "For the promise is for you and for your children" (v. 39). Peter was addressing *Jews*, who were used to *children* being *included in the covenant*. How would they interpret what he had said?

WILLIAM: I could show you a different approach to this passage, which would avoid the conclusion that this continues the promise made to Abraham.

PASTOR COWAN: I suppose all anti-paedobaptists could, but that isn't the point. The question is, how would Peter's words be understood by a people who had lived all their lives under a covenant in which children were included—children who, as a result, were to be given the seal of the covenant? *How would the Jews* understand Peter's words?

WILLIAM: I suppose they would understand them to include their children.

PASTOR COWAN: There would be no other interpretation for them to make. And there is none we can make, if we are sincerely interested in pursuing the truth.

WILLIAM: Are there any more examples?

PASTOR COWAN: Please read 1 Corinthians 7:14.

WILLIAM: "For the unbelieving husband is made holy because of his wife, and the unbelieving wife is made holy because of her husband. Otherwise your children would be unclean, but as it is, they are holy." I've heard a very convincing take on this, though, which proves that this verse is not referring to infant baptism.

PASTOR COWAN: And what is that?

WILLIAM: That *holy* here means "legitimate."

PASTOR COWAN: Well, what if both parents were unbelievers; what would this mean about their children?

WILLIAM: It would mean that their children would not be legitimate. But what does that mean?

PASTOR COWAN: Very clearly, it means that the children would be ceremonially unclean and not entitled to the seal of the covenant. This needed no explanation for the Corinthians, and it's clear to anyone else who is willing to understand it. It is one of those passages that take for granted that children have not been cut off from the covenant.

WILLIAM: But isn't it strange that we have to take these things for granted? That out of all the baptisms that are recorded, there are no clear examples of the baptism of children?

PASTOR COWAN: Not if you remember that when we were discussing the method of baptism, you found only a few cases of the baptisms of even adults.

Let me ask you another question. If one of our missionaries received a husband and wife into the church; and, when he baptized them, he also baptized their children (children too young to act on their own), how would this baptism be reported?

WILLIAM: He might say that he had baptized the man and his entire family.

PASTOR COWAN: And what does Acts 16:15 say?

WILLIAM: "And after she [Lydia] was baptized, and *her household* as well, she urged us, . . . 'Come to my house and stay.'"

PASTOR COWAN: What about verse 33?

WILLIAM: "And he [the jailer] took them the same hour of the night and washed their wounds; and he was baptized at once, he and *all his family.*"

PASTOR COWAN: And also 1 Corinthians 1:16.

WILLIAM: "I did baptize also the *household* of Stephanas. Beyond that, I do not know whether I baptized anyone else."

These mentions of baptizing households do seem compelling. But this may have referred only to those who could act on their own. As far as the jailer, Acts 16:32 says, "They spoke the word of the Lord to him and to all who were in his house." This implies that the members of his household could understand for themselves.

PASTOR COWAN: Does that include infants?

WILLIAM: Only if they understood what the apostles were saying.

PASTOR COWAN: Isn't there anything this could mean *besides* that the apostles spoke to everyone in the house who was capable of understanding? You should remember that we considered this when we looked at the verse, "Whoever does not believe is condemned already" (John 3:18). Assuming that there were some people in the household who could understand and some who could not, wouldn't it still be proper to use the language that this verse uses?

WILLIAM: Yes, if you follow the reasoning that this wording does not include babies since they weren't capable of understanding.

PASTOR COWAN: And by the law of probability, isn't it likely that there were babies in *some* of those households?

WILLIAM: I admit, there probably were.

PASTOR COWAN: So now we have considered the question, and here is what we have learned. I have showed you "a positive command," a "the LORD God said," giving children a place in the covenant, and requiring that the seal of the covenant be applied to them. We have learned that the covenant with Abraham was the covenant of *grace*. The law established in this covenant was never fulfilled or repealed—and of course, it couldn't be by its very nature. Nothing other than a "the LORD God said" command would be sufficient evidence that a law of God had been repealed.

Not only does no such command exist, but nothing from the Bible even implies that this law had been repealed. On the contrary, the New Testament provides very conclusive evidence that it was assumed—taken for granted, in fact—that the law was still in operation, along with the covenant of grace.

We have also considered the baptisms of several households. Taken in conjunction with everything else we have learned, these examples make it practically certain that baptism—which corresponds with circumcision, the seal of the covenant under the Old Testament—was performed on the infant children of believing parents. What more can you ask for in the way of proof?

WILLIAM: You've presented the subject to me in a new light. I have to admit, your argument seems indisputable—convincing, even. You have supplied the "positive command" and the "the LORD God said" that I demanded.

Now I understand why you insisted that I quote the rest of the passage from Revelation. I now agree that neglecting infant baptism is *taking away* from the instructions God has given us. Christian parents are definitely overlooking their duty if they do not follow this divine command.

INDEX OF SCRIPTURE

ABOUT THE AUTHOR

James McDonald Chaney graduated from the William Jewell College in Missouri and received a Masters degree from King College in Tennessee. He went on to receive a Doctor of Divinity degree from Princeton Theological Seminary in New Jersey and was ordained in 1858 by the Lafayette Presbytery of the Presbyterian Church, Missouri. He served as pastor and preacher at several churches in Missouri and was the president of the Elizabeth Aull Female Seminary in Lexington, Missouri, the Kansas City Ladies' College in Independence, Missouri, and the Independence Academy of Missouri.

William the Baptist, his most popular work, was originally published in 1877 and has been reprinted by several publishers.

ABOUT THE EDITOR

Ron Evans received his BA in psychology at Auburn University and his Master of Divinity from Westminster Theological Seminary. He founded The Mustard Seed Christian Bookstore in Pennsylvania, which during his 35 years of ownership grew into four stores.

Ron has served as an elder and chairman of the Church of the Savior and has been on the board of directors of Eastern University where he is also chairman of the Student Development Committee, a member of the Wayne Business Association, and on the board of directors of the National Bible Association.

Contact Ron at TheSeed1@msn.com.